KU-503-519

ONTENTS

A GUIDE TO

AN INSPECTOR CALLS

RUTH COLEMAN
WITH TONY BUZAN

Hodder & Stoughton

Cover photograph ©: John Haynes, Royal National Theatre production of
An Inspector Calls at the Garrick Theatre, London (tel: 0171 494 5085)
Mind Maps: Ann Jones
Illustrations: Karen Donnelly

ISBN 0 340 74763 3

First published 1999
Impression number   10 9 8 7 6 5 4
Year   2002 2001

The 'Teach Yourself' name and logo are registered trade marks of
Hodder & Stoughton Ltd.

Typeset by Transet Limited, Coventry, England.
Printed in Great Britain for Hodder & Stoughton Educational, a division of
Hodder Headline Plc, 338 Euston Road, London NW1 3BH

There are five important things you must know about your brain
and memory to revolutionize
the way you study:

◆ how your memory
  ('recall') works *while* you are learning
◆ how your memory works *after* you have finished learning
◆ how to use Mind Maps – a special technique for helping you
  with all aspects of your studies
◆ how to increase your reading speed
◆ how to prepare for tests and exams.

Recall during learning
– THE NEED FOR BREAKS

When you are studying, your memory
can concentrate, understand and
remember well for between 20 and 45
minutes at a time. Then it needs a break.
If you carry on for longer than this
without a break your memory starts to
break down. If you study for hours non-stop, you will remember
only a small fraction of what you have been trying to learn, and
you will have wasted hours of valuable time.

So, ideally, *study for less than an hour*, then take a five to ten
minute break. During the break listen to music, go for a walk, do
some exercise, or just daydream. (Daydreaming is a necessary
brain-power booster – geniuses do it regularly.) During the break
your brain will be sorting out what it has been learning, and you
will go back to your books with the new information safely
stored and organized in your memory banks. We recommend
breaks at regular intervals as you work through the Literature
Guides. Make sure you take them!

Recall after learning
– THE WAVES OF YOUR MEMORY

What do you think begins to happen to your
memory straight after you have finished learning something?
Does it immediately start forgetting? No! Your brain actually
increases its power and carries on remembering. For a short
time after your study session, your brain integrates the
information, making a more complete picture of everything it
has just learnt. Only then does the rapid decline in memory
begin, and as much as 80 per cent of what you have learnt can
be forgotten in a day.

However, if you catch the top of the wave of your memory,
and briefly review (look back over) what you have been
studying at the correct time, the memory is stamped in far more
strongly, and stays at the crest of the wave for a much longer
time. To maximize your brain's power to remember, take a few
minutes and use a Mind Map to review what you have learnt
at the end of a day. Then review it at the end of a week, again
at the end of a month, and finally a week before your test or
exam. That way you'll ride your memory
wave all the way there – and beyond!

The Mind Map ®
– A PICTURE OF THE WAY YOU THINK

Do you like taking notes? More importantly, do you like having to
go back over and learn them before tests or exams? Most
students I know certainly do not! And how do you take your
notes? Most people take notes on lined paper, using blue or
black ink. The result, visually, is boring! And what does *your*
brain do when it is bored? It turns off, tunes out, and goes to
sleep! Add a dash of colour, rhythm, imagination, and the whole
note-taking process becomes much more fun, uses more of your
brain's abilities, and improves your recall and understanding.

A Mind Map mirrors the way your brain works. It can be used
for note-taking from books or in class, for reviewing what you
have just studied, and for essay planning for coursework and
in tests or exams. It uses all your memory's natural techniques
to build up your rapidly growing 'memory muscle'.

You will find Mind Maps throughout this book. Study them, add some colour, personalize them, and then have a go at drawing your own – you'll remember them far better! Stick them in your files and on your walls for a quick-and-easy review of the topic.

HOW TO DRAW A MIND MAP

1 Start in the middle of the page. This gives your brain the maximum room for its thoughts.
2 Always start by drawing a small picture or symbol. Why? Because a picture is worth a thousand words to your brain. And try to use at least three colours, as colour helps your memory even more.
3 Let your thoughts flow, and write or draw your ideas on coloured branching lines connected to your central image. These key symbols and words are the headings for your topic. Start like the Mind Map on page 7.
4 Then add facts and ideas by drawing more, smaller, branches on to the appropriate main branches, just like a tree.
5 Always print your word clearly on its line. Use only one word per line.
6 To link ideas and thoughts on different branches, use arrows, colours, underlining, and boxes (see page 21).

HOW TO READ A MIND MAP

1 Begin in the centre, the focus of your topic.
2 The words/images attached to the centre are like chapter headings; read them next.
3 Always read out from the centre, in every direction (even on the left-hand side, where you will have to read from right to left, instead of the usual left to right).

USING MIND MAPS

Mind Maps are a versatile tool – use them for taking notes in class or from books, for solving problems, for brainstorming with friends, and for reviewing and working for tests or exams – their uses are endless! You will find them invaluable for planning essays for coursework and exams. Number your main branches in the order in which you want to use them and off you go – the main headings for your essay are done and all your ideas are logically organized!

Super speed reading

It seems incredible, but it's been proved – the faster you read, the more you understand and remember! So here are some tips to help you to practise reading faster – you'll cover the ground more quickly, remember more, and have more time left for both work and play.

◆ First read the whole text (whether it's a lengthy book or an exam or test paper) very quickly, to give your brain an overall idea of what's ahead and get it working. (It's like sending out a scout to look at the territory you have to cover – it's much easier when you know what to expect!) Then read the text again for more detailed information.
◆ Have the text a reasonable distance away from your eyes. In this way your eye/brain system will be able to see more at a glance, and will naturally begin to read faster.
◆ Take in groups of words at a time. Rather than reading 'slowly and carefully' read faster, more enthusiastically.
◆ Take in phrases rather than single words while you read.
◆ Use a guide. Your eyes are designed to follow movement, so a thin pencil underneath the lines you are reading, moved smoothly along, will 'pull' your eyes to faster speeds.

Preparing for tests and exams

◆ Review your work systematically. Cram at the start of your course, not the end, and avoid 'exam panic'!
◆ Use Mind Maps throughout your course, and build a Master Mind Map for each subject – a giant Mind Map that summarizes everything you know about the subject.
◆ Use memory techniques such as mnemonics (verses or systems for remembering things like dates and events).
◆ Get together with one or two friends to study, compare Mind Maps, and discuss topics.

AND FINALLY...

Have *fun* while you learn – it has been shown that students who make their studies enjoyable understand and remember everything better and get the highest grades. I wish you and your brain every success! (Tony Buzan)

HOW TO USE THIS GUIDE

This guide assumes that you have already read *An Inspector Calls*, although you could read 'Background' and 'The story of *An Inspector Calls*' before that. It is best to use the guide alongside the play. You could read the 'Who's Who?' and 'Themes' sections without referring to the play, but you will get more out of these sections if you do refer to it to check the points made in these sections, and especially when thinking about the questions designed to test your recall and help you to think about the play.

THE DIFFERENT SECTIONS

The 'Commentary' section can be used in a number of ways. One way is to read a section of the play, and then read the Commentary for that section. Keep on until you come to a test section, test yourself – then have a break! Alternatively, read the Commentary for a section of the play, then read that section in the play itself, then go back to the Commentary. Find out what works best for you.

'Topics for discussion and brainstorming' gives topics that could well feature in exams or provide the basis for coursework. It would be particularly useful for you to discuss them with friends, or brainstorm them using Mind Map techniques (see p. vi).

'How to get an "A" in English Literature' gives valuable advice on what to look for in a text, and what skills you need to develop in order to achieve your personal best.

'The exam essay' is a useful 'night before' reminder of how to tackle exam questions, and 'Model answer' gives an example of an A-grade essay and the Mind Map and plan used to write it.

The questions

Whenever you come across a question in the guide with a star ✪ in front of it, think about it for a moment. You could even jot down a few words in rough to focus your mind. There is not usually a 'right' answer to these questions: it is important for you to develop your own opinions if you want to get an 'A'. The 'Test yourself' sections are designed to take you about 10–20 minutes each – which will be time well spent. Take a short break after each one.

PAGE NUMBERS

Page references are to the Samuel French 1945 edition. Most other published versions available in the UK can be substituted, however.

KEY TO ICONS

Themes

A **theme** is an idea explored by an author. Whenever a theme is dealt with in the guide, the appropriate icon is used. This means you can find where a theme is mentioned just by flicking through the book. Go on – try it now!

Community and the individual

Conscience and guilt

Respectability and hypocrisy

Time

Responsiblity and power

STYLE AND LANGUAGE

This icon is used whenever the guide focuses on the author's choice of words and **imagery** (a kind of word picture used to make an idea come alive) and the overall way in which the play is organized.

20th CENTURY BRITAIN

Technical and economic progress. Power shifts to industrialists from land-owners. New urban working class grows

1906 Liberal majority. Women's Suffrage movement becomes active.

1908 Old age pensions introduced.

1909 First cross-channel flight

Labour exchanges established **1910**

Henry Ford concentrates on producing Model-T, Beginning of cheap cars

1911

National Insurance and Unemployment Insurance introduced

1912 Titanic sinks

Great British Rail Strike

WORLD WAR I **1914 - 1918**

1920 First university degrees open to women

Women enfranchised **1928**

1939 - 1945 WORLD WAR II - huge loss of life. Major cities destroyed. Clothes and food rationed. All fit men conscripted to fight

Labour victory in General Election. Britain sets about massive rebuilding programme. **1945**

1947 School leaving age raised. Priestley writes "An Inspector Calls"

1948 National Health Service established

1950 Gas electricity and railways nationalised.

Old and new orders

An Inspector Calls is set in 1912, and was written in 1947.
During the years between these dates, Britain was involved in
two wars which turned the world upside down and disrupted
the old order for ever.

Already an established writer, playwright and broadcaster,
particularly known for his morale-boosting wartime broadcasts,
Joseph Boynton Priestley used his reputation to explore the
clash of the old and the new orders. He drew attention to the
complacency of Britain after the Industrial Revolution and
before the World Wars, and supported the gathering Socialist
movement which began to see the world as a place where
responsibility for all is shared by all. This contrasted with the
view that each person is only responsible for him or herself.

Priestley sought to warn his audiences of the threat posed by
carrying on as before, putting too much faith in outdated values
and institutions. The first audiences of *An Inspector Calls* were
receptive to new ideas which could mend the misery and
deprivation of a war-torn nation. This was a society hungry to
find ways forward to a better future. The contrast between these
views continues in present-day British party politics. In 1987,
just three years after Priestley died, Margaret Thatcher who was
Prime Minister at the time said, 'There is no such thing as
society.' ✪ Do you agree?

All in the mind

Priestley, like other thinkers of his time, was also extremely
interested in the brain and the way the mind works.
Psychologists such as Freud and Jung, who had first explored
and put forward ideas about why we are like we are, what
motivates us, and how life events mould our character, were
researching and writing at this time. They were to make
concepts such as the IQ (intelligence quotient), the ego,

psychoanalysis and therapy a part of modern daily life. This interest in the workings of the brain has led, among other things, to the development of the learning principles behind this study guide.

Priestley's play demonstrates his fascination with the mind as he systematically makes the mysterious Inspector penetrate the private thoughts and consciences of a few privileged characters.

A *crafty overview*

Priestley cleverly moves us and his characters through a jolly gathering dominated by the pompous Arthur Birling to unearth events that reveal some of the worst aspects of their characters. His play is chilling and full of suspense. The pattern the plot is taking becomes apparent to us early on, which makes it all the more exciting as we realize that each character is implicated, and that the scale of each one's responsibility is greater than that of the last. By Act 3, when only Eric is yet to be challenged, we have been given such a clear idea of the extent of his guilt that an explanation from him is unnecessary. The loop of revelations is complete and Eric's guilt is used to explore the hypocrisy of the Birling parents.

The suspense is not over when the Inspector leaves – two more twists of the plot take place and broaden the scope of the issues raised during the investigation. Is the Inspector a ghoul of the imagination? Before we have time to work this out, the telephone rings menacingly and the loop begins again.

Way back when

Look at the summary of some key events which took place in the first half of the twentieth century.

?   Would you have liked to have been the age you are now in 1912? Why?

?   Jot down some of the differences between life in the first and second halves of the twentieth century.

take a break before some serious business

THE STORY OF AN INSPECTOR CALLS

A CELEBRATION

The prosperous Birling family have just enjoyed a dinner to celebrate the engagement of the young Sheila Birling to Gerald Croft, son of a leading manufacturer and rival to Arthur Birling. As the pompous Birling is giving out advice to his future son-in-law, a police inspector calls with the news that a young woman has poisoned herself and died.

TWO DISMISSALS

The Inspector questions the reluctant Birling, who soon admits that he once employed the girl but dismissed her after she was seen as a ringleader in a strike for a wage increase. He refuses to see this action as a factor contributing to her suicide, and the Inspector moves on to question Sheila. She admits to having the girl dismissed from the dress shop where she had found a new job and where the Birling family have an account and much influence. The reason for Sheila's complaint was simply jealous rage because the girl was pretty and looked better than Sheila in a dress that she wanted. Sheila, unlike her father, is thoroughly ashamed of herself, and does feel partly responsible for the woman's death.

GERALD AND MRS BIRLING INVOLVED

The Inspector's questioning moves on to Gerald Croft. It is soon revealed not only that he knew the dead woman but that she had been his mistress for a time – a revelation that shocks the family but confirms Sheila's suspicions about his behaviour. She breaks off the engagement.

The Inspector turns his attention to Mrs Birling. At first denying any involvement, she eventually admits refusing help to the dead girl partly because she had used the Birling name in her appeal to Mrs Birling's charitable committee. The Inspector makes Mrs Birling reveal that the dead girl was pregnant, had refused to marry the baby's father and would take no more stolen money from him. Mrs Birling claims that she persuaded her committee to turn down help because the girl was a liar, and because the baby's father was responsible for the pregnancy, he should marry her, and should be punished as an example to other young men.

ERIC IS EXPOSED

It is soon revealed that the Birling's own son Eric is the drunken idler responsible for the pregnancy. He has also stolen the money to provide for his mistress from his own father's business. Although angry, the Birling parents change their tune – they wonder instead how to cover up the incident to prevent a scandal that could tarnish their reputation and squash Birling's hope of a knighthood. Sheila and Eric are shocked that their parents concentrate on this rather than reflecting on their own guilt.

THE PLOT TWISTS AND TURNS

Soon after the Inspector leaves, Sheila suggests that he was not a policeman at all. This prompts the arguing family to make claims and counter-claims that they knew he was a fake all along.

Gerald returns from a walk and puts forward the idea that since no two people saw the photograph of the girl at the same time, perhaps there were several girls. They telephone the hospital to learn that no one has been admitted and died. The Birling parents and Gerald recover their earlier good spirits and make light of the evening but Eric and Sheila are horrified at their lack of remorse. The play closes with a phone call from the police to say that a girl has just died from poisoning at the hospital and an inspector will be calling to ask some questions.

now you know what's what, take a break before finding out who's who

ACT 1

- Family celebrate engagement
- Inspector calls
- Mr Birling questioned
- Sheila questioned
- Gerald about to confess

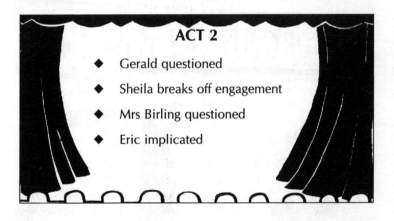

ACT 2

- Gerald questioned
- Sheila breaks off engagement
- Mrs Birling questioned
- Eric implicated

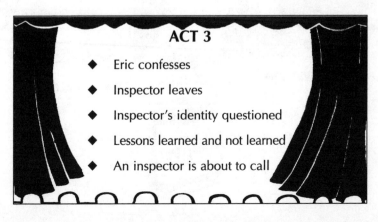

ACT 3

- Eric confesses
- Inspector leaves
- Inspector's identity questioned
- Lessons learned and not learned
- An inspector is about to call

DECLINE AND FALL OF EVA SMITH

Leads strike; fired by Birling

Sheila gets her sacked from Milwards dress shop

Gerald sets her up in a flat and has an affair with her

Eric uses her for sex

Refused help by Mrs Birling's charity

Suicide

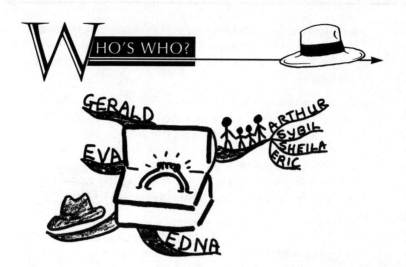

Make a copy of this Mini Mind Map, add to it as you get to know the characters, and then compare it with the one on p. 21.

Arthur Birling

A heavy-looking, rather portentous man in his middle fifties, with fairly easy manners but rather provincial in his speech

Arthur Birling can be viewed in several ways. He is head of the family, head of the firm, and represents the values of Edwardian Britain. The first set directions and scene-setting instructions of the play make this very clear. As head of the family he hands around the decanter of port, makes speeches and presides over the gathering.

Arthur Birling is a traditionalist. He has worked hard, made his fortune, married above himself, taken on all sorts of civic duties, and is very pleased with himself. The last thing he wants is any change which could affect his new-found status. Evidence of this appears frequently, from his buying port from the same supplier as the socially superior Crofts, to his concern with the possible effect of scandal on his chances of a knighthood. As a former Lord Mayor and a magistrate, he believes himself to be right about everything, and is blind to much of what goes on – such as Eric's drinking. In his self-made wealth in which moderate alcohol consumption is a symbol of status, he fails to see the dangers of alcohol, and is too liberal in encouraging drinking.

The speech Arthur Birling makes to the initially happy gathering (*'I'm delighted about this engagement ...'*) makes claims and predictions which may have been valid once, but which will be proven wrong and shaken down for ever. Here we must remember that the play was written some time after the year in which it is set. This allows Priestley to use Birling to show the audience how wrong these views were.

Although Birling is 'blind' in some ways, in other cases he simply turns a blind eye. He must know that Alderman Meggarty is a lewd and lecherous man, and that the respectable married men Eric refers to can be seen with *fat old tarts round the town*. Perhaps Birling even goes to such women himself. In this sense he is typical of his time, and the values and beliefs that go with it – an era of double standards, when there is one rule for men of his class and another for everyone else. Eva Smith is the victim of this dual standard. To a certain extent so is Birling's own son. When Birling asks Eric why he did not come to him for help when he got into a mess, the reply is, *'Because you're not the kind of father a chap could go to when he's in trouble.'*

Priestley has made Birling and his wife the mouthpieces of all he criticizes in the play. He also makes this authoritarian character learn absolutely nothing either as a father, an employer or in a moral sense. Birling never shows any human sorrow or compassion for the dead girl with which his family is so entwined. He does not look at himself to see if and how he could have been a better father. Worst of all, he can only see a young girl's downfall, for which his family has been largely responsible, as an obstacle to his knighthood. All he cares about is preserving his position in society, and covering up any scandal which could threaten it. He is morally very small.

Gerald Croft

An attractive chap about thirty, rather too manly to be a dandy but very much the easy well-bred young man-about-town

Sheila's fiancé is very happy with his life. He is the son of a respected local manufacturer, Sir George, and his wife Lady Croft. He does not have to show off his social status, unlike his future father-in-law, because he has known it all his life and takes it for granted. Unlike Eric, he can take his drink, has been educated to be polite at all times, and is really rather relaxed about life. Unlike Eric he is treated man-to-man by Birling – as an equal, not a wayward child.

At the time when the play is set a courting couple from an upper or middle class family would not consider sex before marriage. However, it was quite acceptable for a young man to visit prostitutes – providing no one found out. Marriage was much more about making a union between people of similar social standing within which children would be raised, and which would be of mutual financial benefit. Gerald is therefore not particularly unusual in keeping a mistress and explaining his absences by his being *awfully busy at the works.*

The family – apart from Sheila – take the revelation of Gerald's affair reasonably well partly for these reasons. Their disapproval is also lessened because he has conducted the affair discreetly, did not make the girl pregnant, and acted initially out of genuine concern for her well being. He is lucky that the girl lets him off the hook so easily when the affair is over – as Sheila puts it with irony, *'That was nice for you.'*

He comes in the middle of the 'sandwich' of guilt presented in the play, and gets off fairly lightly from the Inspector's judgment with the comment, *'he at least had some affection for her and made her happy for a time.'* He remains rather neutral over the community-individual issue, and so it is perhaps a little surprising that Priestley lets him off so lightly. Perhaps the fact of the affair and the affection with which it was conducted foreshadows the more liberal times to which we have since become accustomed.

Gerald shows intelligence when he works out the possible explanation of the 'crime' never having taken place. The Birling family is lucky to have him thinking for them. He is the moderate voice in what the gathering learn, somewhere between the poles represented by the Birling parents and their children. He will not forget, but will probably be less drastically affected than Eric and Sheila.

Now and then

?   Mind Map all the important public offices Arthur Birling holds or has held.

?   How sound is Arthur Birling's analysis of current affairs?

?   How does Gerald lie to Sheila?

take a break before meeting someone more willing to learn than Arthur Birling

Sheila Birling

A pretty girl in her early twenties, very pleased with life and rather excited

Sheila is the character who develops most in the play. From the opening description of her, followed by the account of her getting Eva Smith the sack – which shows her up as a spoilt, self-centred brat, she learns to admit to her shameful behaviour, and to take responsibility for her actions. She faces up to unpleasant truths about her future husband and family, and learns lessons which will influence her for ever.

She is not a particularly interesting or likeable character at the start of the play, but the key to her personality change – her keen intuition – is soon apparent. She knows Gerald is lying to her about his whereabouts during the previous summer, and she is not blind to Eric's drinking. When she has admitted her role in Eva Smith's undoing, her moral integrity grows. She first feels that the Inspector is strange, *real* as she puts it, at the start of Act 2, and when her mother re-enters, *quite out of key with the little scene which has just passed*, Sheila immediately feels this. She does not gloss over her temper tantrum and feelings of jealousy; she faces up to what she has done and to her guilt, unlike her parents who try to explain it away and justify it.

Sheila is also very quick to tune in to the Inspector's inquiry and almost becomes a partner in it. Apart from her father, who has been questioned before her, she does not know what each of the others has done, but she is quick to absorb the fact of the suicide and feel sorry for the dead girl. When she begins to suspect her own part in the death and recognizes the photograph, her reaction is not to pretend she does not recognize the girl, as her parents do. It is to run from the room, almost involuntarily, in horror at what she has done. Coming to terms with this, she is not prepared to help Gerald conceal his role in the matter from the Inspector because she knows intuitively that such an effort would be futile. Her support for the Inspector during Acts 2 and 3 frequently draws comments of outrage from her parents, such as: *'please be quiet, Sheila'*; *'Sheila, don't talk nonsense'*; *'You're behaving like an hysterical child'*; and, *'Really, from the way you children talk, you might be wanting to help him* [the Inspector] *instead of us.'*

Sheila also proves herself to be a match for Gerald. When she breaks off the engagement after the revelations about his involvement with the dead girl, it is as much because she realizes she hardly knows the real Gerald, as because of his lies and infidelity. She is interested in his moral integrity, how he has learned from the experience, rather than dwelling on the deed itself, which she can forgive. It is only when he is honest and shows signs of having learned lessons himself that her respect for him begins to be restored.

Supported by Eric in criticizing her parents throughout Act 3, Sheila is the main force for presenting what the gathering should be feeling about the dead girl – how their consciences should be responding. By the end of the play she may still be a pretty girl in her early twenties, but she is more serious and has learned compassion for her fellow human beings.

Sybil Birling

About fifty, a rather cold woman and her husband's social superior

Sybil Birling is a rather grey woman – dull, uninteresting, with not a spark of any really likeable quality – and that's before we are introduced to her mean-spirited and prejudiced attitude. She presides coolly over the engagement dinner, correcting her husband when he shows lack of breeding and indulging him when he wants to make a speech. Like her husband, she is typical of her time and social class, and is jointly responsible for spoiling and patronizing her children.

Mrs Birling is absent for most of Act 1, during the revelations about her husband and daughter, although her husband will have briefed her off-stage. At this point in the play and during Gerald's confession we cannot imagine that such a paragon of Edwardian virtue will be revealed as such an unrepentant and heartless woman. Despite Sheila's warnings, Mrs Birling continues to patronize the Inspector, and threaten him with rank and social connections.

She then demonstrates that she has chosen not to notice the real Eric, the one who drinks, or the lewd behaviour of her husband's associates. She only sees what fits her respectable values and ignores the truth and contradictions of her system of beliefs. This is keenly demonstrated when she is questioned. She at first pretends not to recognize Eva Smith, and then accuses her of *claiming elaborate fine feelings and scruples that were simply absurd in a girl in her position*, as if a pregnant girl with no money could not have feelings or morals. She later says of the dead girl who tried to protect her son and would take no more stolen money, *'As if a girl of that sort would ever refuse money!'*

The Inspector's accusations of heartlessness have no effect on her, even though Sheila backs him up with showy emotional outbursts. When she feels the screws tighten down on her, all she can do is shift the blame onto the man who made the girl pregnant, little realizing what Sheila and the audience are beginning to suspect – that this man is in fact her own son.

Even when Eric has confessed, Mrs Birling still tries to deny Eric's drinking, and avoids looking at her own role in damaging her children, and in the girl's death. She has done her duty by her own belief system, refuses to learn anything, and is quick to join in the cover-up which will spare her the trouble of looking at herself critically. She is even conceited enough to claim to be *the only one of you who didn't give in to him* (the Inspector). She shows herself to be morally reprehensible, and by her lack of action to be even smaller in moral stature than her husband.

First impressions

? What do you think Arthur Birling said to his wife about the Inspector's visit before she enters in Act 2?

? How do you think an actor playing Sybil Birling would create the impression that Priestley asks for – that she is 'her husband's social superior?'

? What similarities or differences are there between mother and daughter?

take a break from the family before you meet the others

Edna

A neatly dressed parlourmaid

Edna's presence makes it clear from the start that the Birlings can afford servants and are thoroughly middle class. She shows the deference expected of someone of her class, and serious matters are not discussed in front of her. She also provides occasional relief from the dramatic tension created by the interplay between the other characters. However, because she answers the door to visitors, whose arrival always creates a sense of anticipation, her ordinariness has the effect of exaggerating the potential menace by contrast.

Eric Birling

In his middle twenties, not quite at ease, half-shy, half assertive

Eric is a bit of a mess. With better parenting he could so easily have turned out better – perhaps like Gerald Croft. He has obviously not been taken seriously by his parents, is still treated like a child and has the accompanying lack of confidence and self-esteem that has driven him to drink. He has not been shown the kind of love and attention that would have enabled him to make his way in the world in a field of his choosing. Rather, we suspect, he has failed despite his expensive education, and has had no real choice but to join his father's business. He is a disappointment to his parents, and probably to himself. Having become a drunk, he has the drunkard's potential to turn nasty, and as good as rapes the girl he soon makes pregnant, completely unaware of his actions at the time.

Because the Birling parents are so awful, we feel less inclined to blame Eric. It should also be noted that his father is very liberal with alcohol – he has set his son a poor example. The way Eric has turned out is not entirely his own fault. Perhaps he is a sensitive soul who has gone wrong, rather than being a complete villain.

Eric's nervousness is first apparent at the dinner table when he laughs for no reason. It is as if he can see through Gerald's lies and the social conventions which conceal the darker forces at work. His disrespect for his father when he tries to stop him making a speech, shows up Birling's pomposity and gives us a laugh. Eric is somewhere else, not a participating member of this apparently happy family.

Birling's speech-making tendencies are not to be suppressed, however, and Eric shows how much more in touch with the world he is than his father when he challenges him about the possibility of war. In a typical put-down, he is told: *'You've a lot to learn yet.'*

That something is amiss with a woman about which we will hear later is made clear after Eric has left the stage with his mother and Sheila and then rejoined the men. Almost immediately afterwards, just before the Inspector enters and the three consider why an Inspector should be visiting, Gerald makes a joke. He says, *'Unless Eric's been up to something'* – a comment which makes Eric very uneasy and prompts him to fill his glass. This incident foreshadows later events.

As the news of Eva Smith's death is related and Birling makes his excuses, Eric is quick to stick up for the girl and her right to try for higher wages. As demonstrated by his understanding that war may break out, he is in touch with the way the world is changing. Soon he admits to having had too much to drink, in order to excuse himself from the gathering. Perhaps the inquiry is reminding him of his own predicament. When the Inspector says that Eric may be needed it confirms to the audience that Eric is hiding something, and that the inquiry is going to extend and develop. ❂ What clues are we given about how it will develop?

Eric is absent from the stage from the end of Act 1 until all but the last moments of Act 2. He has missed the confessions of Gerald and his mother. When he returns to realize that everyone knows what he has done, he is a miserable figure. Like his sister he does not try to justify himself – he is prepared to admit his huge faults and appalling behaviour and all the sordid details. Although he knows that he has acted very badly, he shows that he did his best to stick by the girl, who was clever enough to see what a silly young fool he was.

Priestley makes us feel Eric's pain when he accuses his mother of murdering her own grandchild. It is a hugely emotional moment, and the highest point of dramatic tension in the play. This moment is broken only by the Inspector's command to both Eric, who is *almost threatening* his mother, and Birling, who is physically restraining Eric, that they should stop.

Despite all that Eric has done, we are glad that he fights back from his parents' scorn and tells them he is ashamed of them. He is also the one to remind his father and the audience of Birling's 'every man for himself' speech. Supported by his sister he sums up and repeats what the Inspector has drawn from them and what they should have learned from it. His acceptance of responsibility, and his view of each of those involved, prompts Sheila to say, *'Eric's absolutely right. And it's the best thing any one of us has said tonight and it makes me feel a bit less ashamed of us.'* This support offers hope for reform in the wayward Eric. He has learned a lot and perhaps received the blow he needed to grow up and start to take more responsibility for himself.

For example

? How do you think Eric would have felt if he had heard Gerald's confession?

? Give some examples of the way Eric's 'queer mood' shows itself before his confession.

? Who said the following?

'But these girls aren't cheap labour – they're people' (Act 1).

'As if a girl of that sort would ever refuse money' (Act 2).

'It's still the same rotten story whether it's been told to a Police Inspector or to somebody else' (Act 3).

give yourself a break between this character sandwich

Inspector Goole

A man in his fifties, dressed in a plain darkish suit of the period

The Inspector who comes to visit is a very cleverly drawn character. As a policeman, he is convincing yet not convincing, aggressive yet gentle. He is always in control and his name is not accidental: 'Goole' is a play on words: the similarly sounding word 'ghoul' means (1) a person morbidly interested in death, and (2) an evil spirit or phantom. Priestley's Inspector is certainly interested in death, is prepared to be morbid and shock if it will elicit a response from the person he is interrogating. He is also a phantom – a fleeting supernatural phenomenon. Even the word 'Inspector' breaks down to sound like 'in-spectre'. He is no evil spirit, however, except that he exposes the evil in others. He is the policeman of conscience.

A man in his fifties may be at his peak of reasoning, mature but clear-thinking. He is plainly and soberly dressed, *and need not be a big man but he creates at once an impression of massiveness, solidity, and purposefulness.* He brings these qualities into the way he conducts his inquiry. He claims to know very little, but expertly draws confessions from the most secretive and hypocritical of people, such as Mrs Birling. It is worth remembering, however, that he has seen a letter and *a sort of diary* in the dead girl's room.

This Inspector has very much the style of a policeman. He *has a disconcerting habit of looking hard at the person he addresses before actually speaking.* This at once unnerves and discomfits a person. He declines to drink on duty, as befits a policeman, which also avoids his being under any obligation to Birling for his hospitality. His sobriety also contrasts with the misuse of alcohol so prevalent in the Birling household.

As a dramatic device, the Inspector plays the role of narrator and unifies the structure of the play. He sums up for us what has happened so far. He also steers the inquiry back on track when it wanders or the family break into explorations of their own altered dynamics. He irritates the Birling parents in particular with his cool comments and questions that usually suggest he is waiting for more, which they usually supply.

Occasionally the Inspector passes an opinion in a most un-policemanlike way. After apparently agreeing with Birling over his handling of the workers' wage crisis he says, '... *it's better to ask for the earth than to take it.'* The challenge implicit in this statement is picked up immediately by Birling who tries to use status to retaliate with a threat. Soon the Inspector suggests that everyone should put themselves in the shoes of girls such as Eva Smith and points out to Gerald that he makes no distinction between respectable citizens and criminals as the privileged classes would.

The Inspector handles Sheila firmly and directly, but not unkindly. They almost become partners in the inquiry as the Inspector unravels her confused emotions for her and presents them to Gerald. He does this because she is facing up to herself and her guilt and shows even at this early stage that she will learn from this experience. Because she has tuned into the Inspector's line of inquiry, and has keen intuition, she suspects the truth about the man – that he is not a real policeman. Yet he is more real in his policing than any other officer she has met. This links to the idea that even though we have a justice system to try crimes, our own internal conscience is more authoritative. This also tips off the audience about the man – they will already have noticed his opinions and thought them out of character for a policeman.

We learn a little of the otherworldly Inspector, the Inspector of conscience, when Mrs Birling enters and refuses to listen to her daughter's entreaties not to be smug and argue with the Inspector. He points out that he makes a greater impression on young people, who are more receptive to him, states that he never takes offence, and later that he does have the power to make people change their minds. He does not shy away from accusing people of lying – both Gerald and Mrs Birling try to stall him after recognizing the girl's photograph.

He becomes tough when he has to. Mrs Birling is so uncooperative and tries to conceal and justify her role so much that he becomes as aggressive as he needs to be to prise the truth from her. He similarly enters into direct confrontation with Birling who tries, a little late in the day, to stop Eric from having a drink before he tells his sorry tale. When, soon after, relations in the family are strained to breaking point, the Inspector commands them to stop, and calms them all down before he sums up.

These factors all contribute to making the Inspector a character so subtle that once he has left and the other characters are desperately trying to make everything all right again, they cannot understand how he became their confessor and drew so much from them. It is only when the final telephone call comes that the mystery is cleared up. The Inspector is a moral force who has made the characters judge themselves. Those who have learned least from the experience will be forced to go through the process again until they face up to their guilt.

Eva Smith

'A nice little promising life there ... and a nasty mess somebody's made of it'

Although we never meet her, Eva Smith is a key character – or characters. As Gerald Croft reasons in the final Act, perhaps she is several women. The point is that it does not really matter.

Eva Smith represents the new age in several important ways. The name 'Eva' means 'first woman', 'Smith' can be taken to mean 'any woman'. Eve was the first woman, and so in many ways is this one. She is one of the first generation to assert herself by asking for more wages and generally behaving in a way that would have been considered unfitting for a woman in the late nineteenth century. Even when she has not been strident or cheeky as a shop assistant she has no power and is dismissed in a world so unjust that a rich girl's tantrum is enough to stop her earning a respectable living. She tries to become financially independent but is forced towards prostitution and ever further from participation in the moral dream-world inhabited by the Birling parents. She is used by privileged young men who like her and have sex with her but marry respectable girls with whom they may not have sex before they marry – neatly pushing the fact of their sexual behaviour under the carpet. Eva Smith is the one to pay the price of Edwardian society's dual standard.

Eva Smith is also there to dispel the notion that the working classes have no principles – a concept that the Mrs Birlings of the world would contest. She is in fact highly principled. She will not accept more money from Eric when she knows it is stolen, and she is big enough to protect him when she meets his mother even though it is at her own huge expense. She is a strong moral force, having chosen not to expose the way she has been treated by Gerald or Eric. A lesser person with low qualities would have exploited either or both of these men for their money.

19

All about Eva

? Make a Mind Map to show the chain of events that takes place in Eva Smith's life.

? How could Eva Smith have handled the interview with Brumley Women's Charity Organisation to her own better advantage?

? How do you think Eva Smith felt in her last days?

break off now you know who's who, and then look at themes

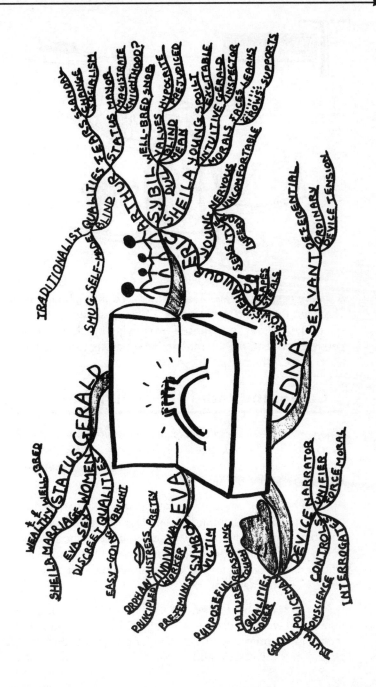

THEMES

A **theme** is an idea developed or explored throughout a work. The main themes in *An Inspector Calls* are shown in the Mini Mind Map above. Test yourself by copying it, adding to it as you read on, and then comparing your results with the full Mind Map at the end of the section.

Community and the individual

'The way some of these cranks talk and write now, you'd think everybody has to look after everybody else, as if we were all mixed up together like bees in a hive – community and all that nonsense' (Arthur Birling, Act 1)

An understanding of what was happening in society in 1912 is helpful to an understanding of the play. The technical and economic developments of the Industrial Revolution had given power to the industrialists, at the expense of the landowners who had held power through agriculture until that time. Society was changed for ever.

People who had worked on the land moved to the cities and a new urban working class was created. The new workplaces, mills and factories were renowned for poor safety and working conditions, low wages, and owners who generally exploited their workers – the John Smiths and Eva Smiths that the Inspector speaks of.

The attitudes prevalent in households such as that of the Birlings would be those of capitalism – the economic system in which trade is controlled by private interests for private profit. Workers who complained about conditions or asked for higher wages would be considered troublemakers. In the economic system preferred by the socialists, trade and industry were owned or controlled by the state for public profit.

At the time when the play is set Britain still had an Empire, consisting of less industrially advanced countries which it governed and exploited for raw materials and cheap labour. Britain's wealth had been made at the expense of the underprivileged at home and abroad, and it fostered the 'every man for himself' attitude that is displayed by Birling and which allows the pampered lifestyle of Sheila and Eric.

The play is set two years before the outbreak of World War I (1914–18), and Birling in particular peddles many of the hopes and aspirations he has for himself and his class as they look forward to a time of unequal prosperity uninterrupted by the tragedy, cost and changing world politics brought about by war. Remember that the play was actually written and performed after World War II, when a war-tired, damaged and poorer Britain emerged to pick up the pieces for the second time. A new mood swept the country – a mood which Priestley's Inspector presents to us. We see him challenge the old order and explore the *hope of a better Britain emerging from the war*, as Priestley himself put it.

A socialist government was voted in when war ended in 1945 and people were ready for a change. People had had enough of hardship. A new sense of community had emerged from pulling together in a common cause. In one of his wartime broadcasts, a modest Priestley said, *'My own personal view, for what it's worth, is that we must stop thinking in terms of property and power and begin thinking in terms of community and creation.'* The 'every man for himself' philosophy was to be ridiculed and denounced in this play. All hope rests with the new generation who are not happy to carry on in the same selfish old way.

Respectability and hypocrisy

'... we're respectable citizens and not criminals' (Gerald, Act 1)

Respectability was of great importance to the upper and middle classes of Victorian and Edwardian Britain, but achieving and preserving it meant maintaining a dual standard. For example, upper class women were protected from sex before marriage, but it was accepted that young men would seek it out. Polite society simply turned a blind eye, and denied that it went on. Look at Mrs Birling's reaction to the revelations about Alderman Meggarty. Prostitutes were available but held in contempt by the same upstanding members of the community who sought their services by night. After marriage, and in Sheila and Gerald's case during courtship, women were supposed to accept that men 'worked hard and late at the office'.

Those who were most deserving were refused help by organizations purporting to be charitable if their actions or predicament did not fit in with the values of the predominant social class. Respectability was so important, especially in the class typified by Mrs Birling, that it was to be preserved at any cost. So important was keeping up appearances, that any indiscretion, any moral deviance in families in particular, was potentially scandalous and had to be suppressed. But again, the double standard – hypocrisy – was the other side of this coin. People with such values were quick to judge, ready to make examples of those who had fallen from grace, ready to make them pay for their crime with loss of social standing, unless of course the scandal was in their own family.

When Eric threatens Birling's knighthood, and the family's good name, instead of the moral lynching he has been promised by his mother before he is linked to the crime, he is viewed with anger and shame as a problem to be hushed up immediately.

Priestley exposes the hypocrisy of the respectable, and gives hope to the upcoming generation. Sheila knows what goes on at the Palace Bar, and about the antics of Alderman Meggarty. She is not prepared to turn a blind eye to Gerald's late stays at the office, and insists on being present through much of the sordid detail of the Inspector's inquiry. As with his presentation of community, Priestley is looking to the young to shake up the values of the old, to build a better community, based on respect for all others as part of a true community, not a class system society.

Responsibility and power

'We don't live alone. We are members of one body. We are responsible for each other. And I tell you that the time will soon come when, if men will not learn that lesson, then they will be taught it in fire and blood and anguish' (the Inspector, Act 3)

Linked to the idea of community versus the individual this is a strong theme in the play. Priestley takes the principles of the class system and applies them to one fictitious family and the woman whose life is affected by them. In a class system, the upper classes with their wealth and influence hold responsibility for most matters connected with the way society is organized. The upper classes therefore control much of what happens to the lower classes. Such power over other people, Priestley argues, should be exercised with great care. *An Inspector Calls* is an examination of what could happen if this power is abused. Just exactly who is responsible for the suicide of a working class girl? Which of these privileged characters is facing up to it, and who will go through real change to take responsibility in future?

The clear message Priestley puts over in the play is that simply being responsible for oneself is not enough. The idea that it is, has kept the Birlings going along as they have done until the Inspector calls. Arthur Birling is made to look ridiculous when he puts forward his philosophy – that *a man has to mind his own business and look after himself.* Priestley shows that anyone holding such a view will eventually have to learn that it is wrong.

Those refusing to learn this lesson, the Birling parents with their old, outdated values, are quick to deny they have any responsibility for others. As Birling says of his involvement in Eva Smith's death, in a manner which is amusing as a dramatic exchange but which shows his irresponsibility, *'... I can't accept any responsibility. If we were all responsible for everything that happened to everybody we'd had anything to do with it would be very awkward, wouldn't it?'* ❷ Why is the Inspector's answer – *'Very awkward'* – ironic?

Later, in response to Birling's reiteration of his public role, the Inspector shows his true view when he replies by saying that public men have *responsibilities as well as privileges.*

Mrs Birling is even less inclined to accept responsibility than her husband. Her view of the world is coloured entirely by her own prejudices and ideas about social class. As for her own role in the suicide, she will *accept no blame for it at all*, and states four times that she blames the father of the baby the girl was carrying. For her, duty and responsibility are two quite separate concepts.

There are several different kinds of irresponsibility shown in the play. Mostly it is displayed by the Birling children. Sheila has been so indulged that she can have a temper tantrum which costs a girl her job, and because of her status, is neither challenged by her mother nor by anyone in the shop. She is quick to learn, however, and the Inspector supports her in wanting to stay and listen to Gerald's confession saying, *'She feels responsible ... And if she leaves us now, she'll be all alone with her responsibility.'*

Eric has clearly had considerable difficulty in even taking responsibility for himself. This shows in his drinking, and there is the suggestion that he has been in trouble before. When his father tells him he must face up to some of the responsibilities he has apparently not learned to take during his student years, he replies, *'Well, we don't need to tell the Inspector all about that do we?'*

Later of course we learn that Eric is not at all in control of himself. Although alcohol is a reason for his bad behaviour it is not an excuse. He is able to admit that drinking can make him turn nasty, that he virtually raped the girl, and that he feels thoroughly ashamed of himself. In his wretchedness it seems that he really has learned a lesson in responsibility.

It is interesting that it does not seem to occur to either parent that the irresponsible attitudes and actions of their children could in any way be connected to their upbringing.

Only Gerald who maintains an easy-going, blow-with-the-wind kind of attitude to life, seems to escape Priestley's accusing finger. That he first made contact with the girl because he felt sorry for her, rescued her from the clutches of Alderman Meggarty, made her happy for a time, shows reasonably appropriate remorse for his actions, and suffers a broken engagement, seems to excuse Gerald from further scrutiny. It could be argued, however, that by giving the poor girl a taste of a better life, he ensures her unhappiness and dissatisfaction after the affair has ended.

Conscience and guilt

'I don't know much about police inspectors – but the ones I have met weren't a bit like you. ... As if – suddenly – there came a real one – at last' (Sheila, Act 2)

Conscience, that inner feeling that checks our behaviour and haunts us with guilt if we do wrong, is the inescapable result of some actions. All the characters (apart from Edna and the Inspector) have something on their conscience, a sense of guilt about how they have treated someone less privileged than themselves. The Birling children are better able to face up to their guilty conscience than their parents. As the Inspector says, coolly, when Mrs Birling has remarked on the considerable impression he has made on Sheila, *'We often do on the young ones. They're more impressionable.'* This Inspector of conscience never takes offence, has the power to extract a confession from even the hardest of hearts, such as Mrs Birling, takes control over who may or may not drink, can call the gathering to order, and lectures and finally passes judgment over them.

Whether they have met the same or a different girl, the Inspector, a ghoulish manifestation of their own consciences, sketches out a possible life and how a person's downfall could result from a string of connections in which a powerless person suffers at the hands of those with power over her.

As the interrogation progresses, the matter of guilt is brought out into the relative safety of the family gathering. Mr Birling thinks his conscience is clear, and blames Eric, but whether he admits it or not, he has a guilty conscience, saying the Inspector *took me by surprise*. Mrs Birling delights in being *the only one of you who didn't give in to him*. Gerald is non-committal as ever, and Sheila and Eric appreciate the irrelevance of the Inspector's true identity. His comment, '*You see, we have to share something. If there's nothing else, we'll have to share our guilt*', is understood by Sheila. When the possibility of the Inspector being a real person is finally disproved, those who cannot face their consciences try to pretend nothing has happened and to carry on as before. But the telephone call at the end of play, the final twist, makes sure that they will not get away with it.

Time

Priestley was very interested in exploring time. It is central to his play *Time and the Conways* and it appears again in *An Inspector Calls*. Note that the play was written in 1947 just after the Second World War, but it is set in 1912, just before the First World War. He uses the hindsight that the passing of time allows to comment on events with **dramatic irony** (where a character or characters on stage are unaware of something important that the audience knows about). The audience's perspective on Arthur Birling's speech about the good times ahead, the supposedly unsinkable *Titanic*, and the impossibility of war, is different from that of the characters he is directly addressing. These characters are meant to be unaware of future events and the lessons they will be forced to learn from them about *blood and fire and anguish*. For the characters, the Inspector's view of the world is an alternative to that presented by Birling, not the certainty that the audience knows it to be.

Priestley directly manipulates time at the end of the play. ✪ Have these characters played out the future? Has a future event taken place after the links have been made in the guilty consciences of the Birlings?

? Make a Mind Map to show the kind of irresponsibility that Eric might have displayed in his *public-school-and-Varsity life.*

? Divide this circle up into a pie to show the proportion of responsibility each character has for Eva Smith's death as you see it.

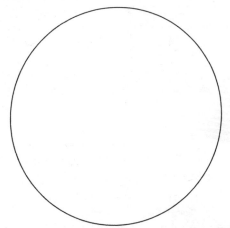

? It could be argued that a further theme, 'Youth and age', is explored in the play. Make notes or a Mind Map on how this could be developed.

now you've looked at themes, take a break before you get some style

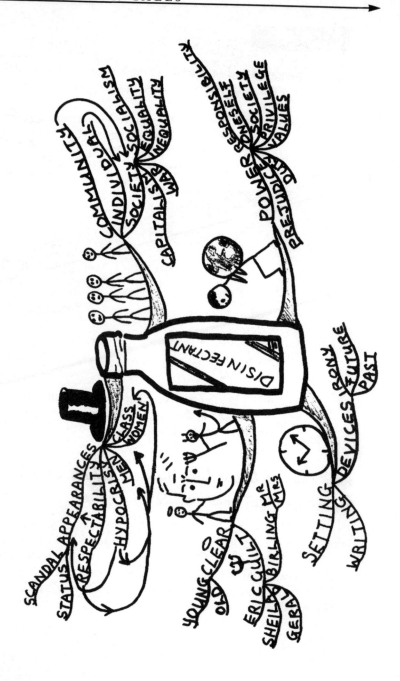

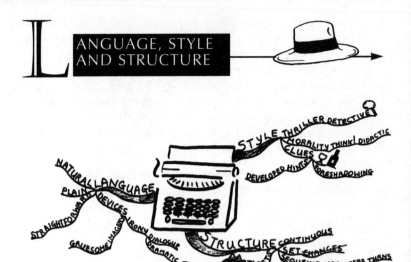

L ANGUAGE, STYLE AND STRUCTURE

The language used in *An Inspector Calls* is natural dialogue.
Unlike plays written in past centuries, for example by
Shakespeare, it has no need for poetic language – the subject
matter and themes do not call for it. It is straightforward, plain-
speaking English such as any well-to-do family might have
spoken in 1912, although the characters do have their own
characteristic language. Birling tends towards the pompous,
Sheila is emotional. ✪ What could you say about the language
of the other characters – the Inspector for example?

Devices

IRONY

Irony occurs when characters express their meaning by saying
the opposite of what they really mean – usually with an
element of bitter humour. This is used mainly by Sheila and the
Inspector. For example, Sheila shows how much Gerald's
infidelity has hurt and angered her by saying, *'That was nice for
you'*, in reply to his comment that the girl had taken the end of
the affair very well.

Early on in the play Arthur Birling comments that being
responsible for everybody *'would be very awkward, wouldn't it?'*

The Inspector replies, *'Very awkward'*. This comment is ironic because on one level the Inspector is pretending to agree with Birling's shallow view, while on a deeper level he actually means that on further examination of events, things will become difficult for Arthur Birling. This also acts as a hint to the audience and can be made to sound quite amusing. Later, when the Inspector is grilling Mrs Birling, he repeats back to her what she has said about who is responsible for the girl's death, knowing full well that she will soon regret her words.

As we have seen, Priestley also uses **dramatic irony** – when the audience knows something of which the characters are unaware. An example of this is when Birling refers to the *Titanic* as *absolutely unsinkable*.

IMAGERY

This refers to the kind of word pictures used to make an idea come alive. Although the language of *An Inspector Calls* is that of simple, direct everyday speech, the Inspector uses gruesome imagery for dramatic effect. He first talks of the poison that *Burnt her inside out, of course*, to the Birling men and Gerald as if they would grasp that fact immediately, when he knows that in fact they would probably not think of the horror of it. He does it to shock.

He also speaks of Eva Smith's *great agony*, tells Sheila that she died *after several hours of agony*, and mentions *what was left of Eva Smith ... a nasty mess*, and her *misery and agony*. He threatens to conjure up the image again to shock the unrepentant Mrs Birling into a confession ('*I wish you'd been with me tonight in the Infirmary. You'd have seen ...*'), but is stopped short by Sheila who has already imagined the horror. Still he uses the image to work on Mrs Birling: '*Her position is now that she lies with a burnt-out inside on a slab.*'

Style and structure

We should look again at the way Priestley uses time. The play is quite short, the action is continuous and the division between acts is really for audience convenience. There are no changes of set or mood to require an interval. The play is an analysis of actions rather than a depiction of the action itself. For example, we do not meet Eva Smith or witness any of the events she experiences.

The play presents a short passage of time which is just long enough for those who are receptive, to face up to their own faults, guilt and responsibility and learn a serious moral lesson. The surprise twist at the end – that after they have discussed it a girl actually does commit suicide – can also be seen as a twist of time. Everything the characters have just been through has been a rehearsal or a dream, a premonition and a practice run of the ordeal they face. ✪ Who do you think will find the questioning most difficult?

The way the Inspector squeezes the characters' confessions from them without presenting much to incriminate them, and the balance between these confessions and the effect they have on the family relationships, is skilfully handled. Every detail has a purpose, and everything is revealed in meticulous order. Each character's action and accompanying guilt is a degree worse than the one which went before. We become aware of this about the time that Gerald is questioned and are in little doubt by the time Mrs Birling is questioned. By the end of Act 2 we know exactly what Eric has done.

The style of a detective thriller (although no imprisonable offence is committed), is mixed with the speculation of a morality play.

Priestley shapes the play by the order in which the Inspector questions the characters. A mnemonic for this is:

A	**Sh**allow	**G**roup	**S**inks	**E**va
Arthur	**Sh**eila	**G**erald	**S**ybil	**E**ric

The order is partly chronological. Birling sacked the girl, starting her on the downward spiral that leads to her death, and so he is questioned first. Sheila's role – getting her sacked from another job – was played out next, and so Sheila is questioned next. The only deviation from this order comes at the end, with Mrs Birling coming before Eric. However, the order could also be seen as reflecting increasing responsibility. ✪ Do you think it does?

These are some of the clues planted by Priestley to form threads of plot which will be picked up and developed later:

♦ the role played by alcohol,
♦ Eric's comment about Sheila's temper,
♦ Sheila's doubts about Gerald's whereabouts the previous summer,
♦ how Birling may receive a knighthood if the family behaves itself,
♦ Eric's half-uttered comment about women and clothes.

✪ What other clues are there?

Many writers have difficulty finding a good ending to their works – not so for Priestley in this play. If you saw a production of the play and did not know the plot, you could well expect it to end after the revelations about Eric have been made and the Inspector leaves. In fact, simply exploring adjustments to family relationships would probably end the play in a satisfactory way. But because Priestley's real intention was to influence his audience towards community responsibility, we have two more very clever twists to take the play away from particular characters, and to make their experience more generally relevant.

We are also made to work quite hard to understand and imagine what else takes place and will go away and think about it afterwards – hopefully to learn something ourselves. This type of play, when the writer is trying to teach the audience something, was common in the drama and literature of the first half of the twentieth century. Such works are called 'didactic', and were written by authors such as *these Bernard Shaws and H. G. Wellses* that Birling refers to so scornfully.

The set

This play is a dream for small theatres. Its plot is so strong, and the action so compelling, that with just seven characters and one set a cheap production is possible. One recent production put the Birlings' house high up on shaky stilts having forced its way up from the wasteland below. ✪ What do you think this represents?

A film of the play was also made in 1957. True to the play, the set was the Birlings' dining room, but each character's confession was 'on location', with Eva Smith, at the Birling works, at the dress shop, at the Palace bar and so on. ✪ Could this have been done on the stage?

Talking of which ...

?   What body language might the actors use to show that they are pleased with themselves at the start of the play?

?   With a partner, improvise the dialogue that might have taken place between Eva Smith and one of the Birlings.

?   Imagine you are producing the play on a shoestring budget. Draw a sketch of how you would design the set.

now you've got some style, take a break to prepare for a running commentary

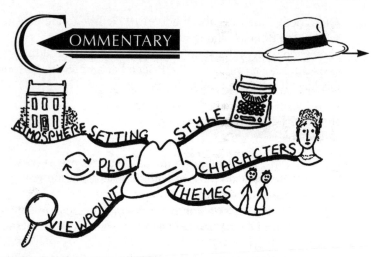

The Commentary divides the play into short sections, beginning with a brief preview which will prepare you for the section and help in last-minute revision. The Commentary comments on whatever is important in the section, focusing on the areas shown in the Mini Mind Map above.

ICONS

Wherever there is a focus on a particular theme, the icon for that theme appears in the margin (see p.xi for key). Look out, too, for the 'Style and language' sections. Being able to comment on style and language will help you to get an 'A' in your exam.

You will learn more from the Commentary if you use it alongside the play itself. Read a section from the play, then the corresponding Commentary section – or the other way around.

QUESTIONS

Remember that when a question appears in the Commentary with a star ✪ in front of it, you should stop and think about it for a moment. And remember to take a break after completing each exercise!

Act 1 (pp. 1–19)

◆ Birling family celebrate Sheila and Gerald's engagement.
◆ Birling makes a speech.
◆ He has a quiet chat with Gerald and Eric.
◆ An Inspector calls with news of Eva Smith's death.
◆ The Inspector questions Birling.
◆ He questions Sheila.
◆ Suspicion falls on Gerald.

The play, involving seven characters, takes place in the Birlings' house in Brumley, an industrial city in the North Midlands. Priestley gives fairly detailed set instructions. We are to be given a first impression that the house is fitting for the family of a *prosperous manufacturer*. This tells us immediately that we are looking at a certain sort of family who can be expected to typify certain attitudes of the period. In 1912 the north of England boasted many new, large suburban houses built by prosperous manufacturers. They had gathered their wealth by producing goods in factories made possible by the development of mass production during and following the Industrial Revolution. Such houses were a status symbol of the successful businessman.

The setting is the dining room. The properties (items of furniture and decoration), or 'props' as they are known, reinforce the Birlings' prosperity. They can afford good quality, such as solid furniture with silver trimmings to complement it. Further information about their social class is revealed in the information that there are *a few imposing but tasteless pictures* on the walls. This suggests that Priestley is snubbing and reinforcing the stereotypical idea that self-made businessmen show off their wealth but do not have the good taste that their social superiors seem to be born with. The atmosphere of the house is conveyed in the set instruction that the *general effect is substantial and comfortable and old-fashioned, but not cosy and home-like.* This statement also conveys a value judgment – that cosiness implies caring and well-being as a kind of socialism at home.

The Birlings are rich enough to have servants, as evidenced by Edna, who makes one of her few brief appearances. All are formally dressed for dinner.

Setting the scene

? What sort of accent would the characters have?
? Some versions of the play include the lighting instruction that: *The lighting should be pink and intimate until the Inspector arrives, and then it should be brighter and harder.* Why do you think this is?
? What do you imagine the rest of the Birlings' house would be like?

take a break before a family celebration

The family celebrate Sheila and Gerald's engagement

(To p. 4, Sheila: Actually I was listening)

The play opens with the Birling family seated around the dining table. They have enjoyed *a good dinner, are celebrating a special occasion, and are pleased with themselves.* It is clear that they have finished dinner, because Edna is clearing away the dessert dishes and brings out the port – a strong wine traditionally taken after dinner. It is the first appearance of alcohol, which often comes up in the play.

We should notice that alcohol is very much a part of Birling life, and a symbol of affluence which is abused by those who are new to it, as we later witness. We can see the tantalus (locked wine cupboard which tantalizingly reveals its contents behind glass doors), champagne cooler, and now the decanter of port. We find out a good deal about Birling and his obsession with social status from the brief exchanges concerning the port.

Attempting to show his social parity with Gerald Croft's father, as he passes around the decanter, Birling opens the dialogue with the comment that Gerald should approve of his taste because, as if by coincidence, it is the same kind as his father has. As a young man self-assured in his social status, Gerald takes it for granted that he will drink good port, and has not needed to know much about it. Arthur Birling, on the other hand, a social climber, tries to learn about it. Sheila reveals that her father knows little about good port and we suspect that he has asked his supplier to give him the same sort that Gerald's father has.

Imagine you do not know the play or are seated in the theatre without a programme. You will wonder what relationships the characters have to each other. Priestley has to find a subtle way to show you this. The exchange has the effect of establishing the relationship between the two and giving some extra information very economically – Gerald is the son of someone Birling looks up to and would like to be equal with.

When Sheila (*gaily, possessively*) asserts her right to influence Gerald by stating that she would not like him to know much about port, there is little doubt that she is amorously attached to him. Mrs Birling has to be coaxed by her husband to take some port – a sign of a well-bred lady. The impression that you are looking at a family gathering is consolidated by Sheila adding encouragement with, *'Yes, go on, Mummy. You must drink our health.'* ✪ Why is this comment a little ironic in view of what happens later?

As the gathering relaxes, Birling again shows his lack of breeding by commenting on the good dinner. Checked by his wife, he makes it clear that the well-bred Gerald is to marry his daughter. Priestley drops a clue that there has been some problem about this situation coming about. Sheila is scolded by her mother for showing some dissatisfaction with Gerald for his considerable absence the previous summer. She is reminded that *men with important work to do sometimes have to spend nearly all their time and energy on their business.* ✪ Why is this statement also ironic?

The kind of squabbling that makes it clear that Eric and Sheila are siblings occurs as Eric's drink problem is hinted at and his social ineptitude is revealed. Birling claims not to mind that Gerald's titled parents are not present to join in the celebration but he is not very convincing. He also assumes that he should make a speech. It would suit his sense of occasion and self-importance to make it to a larger gathering. Eric rather deflates his father's pomposity and perhaps makes the audience laugh when he suggests that he need not make a speech.

But Birling is not to be deprived of his opportunity to reflect on his good fortune. ❂ Why is it ironic that he tells Eric that when he has a daughter of his own, he will understand why it is such a happy night? He explains that he is delighted to have Gerald as a son-in-law. Not we suspect because he is Sheila's choice, but more because it assists him in his social climbing, and may mean a business alliance which will help to achieve his ultimate business aim – *lower costs and higher prices*. Again his want of good manners is checked by Mrs Birling, who reminds him that business talk is not appropriate at the dinner table. Eric shows his lack of respect by having to be told to rise to drink the toast, doing so noisily and then teasing his sister in a way that **foreshadows** (indirectly warns of things to come) her 'crime' against Eva Smith, *'She's got a nasty temper sometimes – but she's not bad really.'*

The mood becomes a little more serious as Sheila's obvious feelings of insecurity about the rather slippery Gerald are made evident. He averts this and makes Sheila *really feel engaged* by producing a ring. As she admires the ring that she is careful of now but will soon give up, her father captures the family's attention in preparation for his speech.

Think about ...

? Do you think Sheila should need a ring to really feel engaged?

? What do you think of the characters so far?

? Why do you think Eric *suddenly guffaws*?

take a break and prepare for a speech

Birling makes a speech

(To p. 5, Gerald shuts the door)

Birling then makes a speech full of dramatic irony. For all his self-importance, just about everything he predicts turns out differently. For the characters on stage, the speech is meant to be the sound voice of age and experience, not really to be argued with. But audiences, whenever the play was seen, have the benefit of hindsight. They know that all the events referred to turn out differently. Priestley has done this deliberately to make Birling and all he represents look rather pathetic, ridiculous and old-fashioned.

He dismisses as *silly pessimistic talk* that the Miners' Strike of 1912 will lead to more labour trouble. He refers to the threat of war as *fiddlesticks* – although the whole world was plunged into war in 1914 – and lists the advances in modes of transport as evidence of increasing prosperity. Although the aeroplane he cites was indeed advancing and the Model-T Ford car was beginning to be mass produced and becoming cheaper, he refers to the *Titanic* as *absolutely unsinkable.* Since this ship actually sank in April 1912, and the play was set in an evening in spring 1912, it is clear to most that the world as Birling knows it is about to come to an end.

To cap it all he refers to what he thinks will be a happy time in about 1940, seven years before the play was first produced, when against his predictions world war breaks out for a second time, and *agitations* between Capital and Labour are anything but resolved. For audiences viewing the play after the break up of the Soviet Union (which took place a further forty years or so after the first showing of the play – an event somehow anticipated by Priestley), there is an added modern relevance.

Birling ends with a reference to the socialist sympathizers, H. G. Wells and Bernard Shaw, doing all the talking but implying they do not know what they are talking about. This would also perhaps be a reverential acknowledgment of Priestley's own contemporaries with whom he has much in common. Eric, here representing the new order, has tried to interrupt several times. It is characteristic of people with attitudes such as Birling's to silence and dismiss other points of view, particularly when they come from a younger person who is actually more in touch with what is really happening in the world. ✪ Have you ever come across this attitude yourself?

Mrs Birling, in the manner of someone experienced in humouring her husband, brings the speech to a close by rising and saying indulgently, *'Yes, of course, dear.'*

Ask yourself ...

? After Birling's speech Mrs Birling tells her son that she wants him for a minute. Why do you think she wants him? Work with a friend, and make up a short conversation that could take place between these characters?

? Why does Gerald open the door for Mrs Birlng, Sheila and Eric, and then close it behind them?

now you've met the family, take a break before they are inspected

Birling has a quiet chat with Gerald and Eric

(To p. 7, Birling: ... benefit of my experience)

The next scene contains several structural features necessary to develop the plot convincingly. We learn what would be at stake for Birling in the event of a scandal, the nature of the trouble to come is revealed apparently unwittingly by Birling, and a clue about Sheila's culpability is dropped by Eric.

Birling enjoys an after-dinner cigar. Like the episode with the port, whether he likes cigars or not he would probably smoke one because it is a further symbol of how pleased he is with himself and his new-found status. Gerald, secure in his standing, prefers cigarettes. In 1912 they were gaining popularity over cigars and were fashionable with the affluent young men of the day. Birling again encourages Gerald to drink.

Having set the scene for a confidential chat, Birling embarrasses Gerald with the suggestion that his mother, Lady Croft, may not wholeheartedly approve of the match. ✪ How do you think Mrs Birling would react if she heard her husband saying this to Gerald? Probably to Gerald's great relief, Birling goes on to suggest that he will soon receive a knighthood.

There are two reasons for Priestley making him say this: it further reinforces the image of Birling as a social climber and it gives the audience the knowledge that he will do almost anything to prevent a scandal which could taint his name or spoil his chances of a knighthood. He is in such a hurry to further improve his social status that he simply cannot resist confiding in Gerald although he would look rather silly if the knighthood fell through. Furthermore it is quite unnecessary to tell him as Gerald is already committed to Sheila. ✪ How wise is it to share expectations such as Birling's with anyone? Again in a way that foreshadows what is to come, Birling states the importance of avoiding the police courts and scandal.

Eric returns and is encouraged to drink more by his father. As the men do what men do, he talks of women doing what women do – talking about clothes. This is highly plausible as planning a trousseau would be part of any wedding plans, although it is really mentioned to give Birling a chance to comment that clothes are for women a *sign or token of their self-respect*. Eric almost relates the incident soon to be revealed but realizes in time that he should not 'rat' on his sister, particularly in front of her fiancé. Although Birling misunderstands, this prepares the ground for the revelations soon to be made about Sheila.

To reinforce the Birling view of the world which is about to turn upside down, and to make his apparently convincing words sound hollow of meaning and validity, Birling again shares the benefit of his experience with Gerald and Eric whether they want to hear it or not. He states that as long as a man is selfish, and only looks out for himself and his family, things will go well for him. He dismisses as nonsense the idea that people should take any kind of community responsibility.

Having thoroughly set the scene (introduced the characters and their attitudes, established what is at stake for them, and presented a philosophical backdrop), Priestley makes the door bell ring while Birling is making his predictions. This has the effect of driving home how wrong he is and how his narrow view will be challenged.

An Inspector calls with news of Eva Smith's death

(To p. 9, Inspector: Otherwise there's a muddle)

Edna shares the information that an Inspector named Goole has arrived – already a clue is planted about the nature of the man, in his unusual name. Birling immediately assumes the visit must be connected to his duties as a magistrate. As if expecting to sign a warrant giving permission to arrest or search somebody, he moves over to the desk and turns on a light above it. This of course has the effect of making the atmosphere change to become more serious and businesslike rather than cosy and after-dinnerlike. The play has shifted gear.

More foreshadowing takes place in the brief exchange before Edna shows the Inspector in. Gerald jokes that Eric might have *been up to something*. With a veiled reminder in the form of a private joke that if such was the case Birling's knighthood could be at risk, Eric takes the lightness out of the joke by behaving guiltily – and helps himself to some more port.

Edna shows the Inspector into the room and onto the stage. Although Priestley gives a physical description of him, it is the impression he makes that is most important. His manner must be one of *massiveness, solidity, and purposefulness*. He will speak *carefully, weightily*, and stare hard at whoever he is speaking to in a way that will make them feel uncomfortable. This is a tried and trusted police technique to make people who are hiding something reveal their guilt. Neither does this Inspector appear to be in any hurry – another technique to make the guilty feel uneasy.

Birling wastes no time in offering alcohol to the Inspector, who, as the only one (apart from Edna) to decline, will have the clearest head. Neither can Birling resist letting the Inspector know how important he is, and how chummy he is with the local police.

The Inspector proceeds to tell the impatient Birling that a young woman has died. He adds quite matter-of-factly and unnecessarily that the disinfectant she used to take her own life, *'Burnt her inside out, of course.'* The way he adds *'of course'* has a chilling effect which clearly shocks the touchy Eric. It conjures up a horrible image, and seems to assume the group will have realized the effect of the poison when they probably have not.

The information that she left a diary suggests that much may be revealed, even though the reason for the Inspector visiting the Birlings has not yet come out. His comment, *'Like a lot of these young women who get into various kinds of trouble'* initially suggests that he will share Birling's attitudes. This apparent collusion may be to coax Birling into talking. When Birling, apparently understanding the reason for the visit, at last says that the *several hundred young women* who work for him keep changing, his tone implies that such changes are their fault rather than his.

The Inspector then shows Birling the photo but prevents Gerald or Eric seeing it. The exchange that follows indicates that they are also somehow implicated, cleverly makes them ill-at-ease, and hints to the audience that their turn will come. Priestley has scattered plenty of clues to the characters' guilt so that the audience is keen to see what happens next. ◐ How important is it to the development of the play that only Birling sees the photo at this stage? To the consternation of all three characters, the Inspector says he likes to work by questioning one person at time. As he says this he is watching Birling and we are confirmed in our impression that it is he who is to be grilled first.

Across

1 (and 1 down)
Two of these took
place in the first half
of the 20th century.
4 Town where everything
takes place.
5 A parlourmaid.
6 Head of the household.

Down

1 (see 1 across)
2 Something Eric might
drink.
3 A well-bred snob?
5 Victim of a
prejudiced society?

(Solution on p. 73.)

The Inspector questions Birling

(To p. 12, Inspector: ... No, she didn't exactly go on the streets)

The photograph having jogged his memory, Birling soon admits that he remembers Eva Smith, that she worked for him, and that he dismissed her. Eric's nervous question, *'Is that why she committed suicide?'* expresses what the audience is thinking – what is the connection between this fact and her death? We go back two years.

Gerald asks if he should leave. This is probably out of a mixture of tact, wanting to avoid this unpleasant situation, and to be identified to the Inspector in order to be told to stay. Again this increases audience curiosity and makes a character more uncomfortable – all tools to build up the suspense.

The Inspector then refers to the chain of events which may have led to the suicide, prompting Birling to reiterate his view that *'If we were all responsible for everything that happened to everybody we'd had anything to do with it would be very awkward.'* 'Awkward' is an interesting choice of word, repeated by the Inspector. It implies that responsibility is only relevant if it contributes to self-advancement; otherwise it is simply an annoyance.

Birling then gives a little detail of the circumstances of Eva Smith's employment and is surprised when the Inspector asks why he refused to increase her wages. For the first time, Birling's irritability gets the better of him and he retorts, *'I don't like that tone.'* The political theme comes up again when it is revealed that the girls were given Hobson's choice (no choice at all) – work for a pittance or work somewhere else, despite there being nowhere else to go. Hearing that the ringleaders were dismissed after the strike, Gerald reveals his sympathy with Birling's capitalist view, and Eric presents us with the socialist alternative.

Birling's irritation is now so great that he makes a couched threat to the Inspector that he will use his influence to quash what he sees as impertinence. Following a humorous exchange about golf, Eric voices Priestley's political views: that captialist society frowns on workers who show initiative and spirit. His father's angry reply shows how ill-suited Eric is to working in his father's factory, and he notes, with what an audience will later see was irony, that Eric should face up to some of life's responsibilities. In preparation for the next interrogation, the information-giving part of Birling's interview comes to a close with his questions about what happened to Eva Smith next.

The Inspector questions Sheila

(To p. 17, Sheila: Oh – why had this to happen?)

Before Sheila's part in the suicide is revealed, Priestley cleverly repeats the details of Birling's involvement and puts them into perspective. Despite his efforts to bring the Inspector's visit to an end, and to protect Sheila from the questioning on her special day, with further threats to the Inspector, the details come out. One of the clues to the Inspector not really being a policeman comes out in his statement, *'She felt she couldn't go on any longer.'* Perhaps this comes from the diary he professes to have read, or perhaps it is an opinion not based on the facts in which the police usually deal.

After a little more gruesome imagery, the finger of suspicion is pointed again at the Birlings and Gerald, who are united in their apparent bewilderment. Birling backtracks on his threats to the Inspector, and is unable to settle things on Sheila's behalf, because she shows the same independence of mind for which Eva Smith was sacked.

Expressions of sympathy and understanding for Eva now come from Sheila as well as Eric. Like Eric she presents the opposite view from her father when she says, *'But these girls aren't cheap labour – they're people.'* Again the Inspector makes what, for a policeman, is an uncharacteristic observation, about putting ourselves in the shoes of those less fortunate than ourselves.

Soon we learn that the poor and lonely Eva Smith changed her name, and got a job in a clothes shop used by Sheila. Despite Birling's anticipating that she got into trouble or didn't do her work properly, we learn that she was a perfectly satisfactory employee, but was dismissed when a customer complained about her. As the stage direction asks for Sheila to appear agitated we suspect that she is this very customer. This is confirmed by Sheila's recognition and shock when she is shown the dead woman's photo. Sheila running out of the room increases the agitation in the remaining three characters. Arthur Birling insists on being the one to go and find her and to tell his wife what is going on. We are reminded that only one person at a time sees the photo and is put under the spotlight of inquiry.

A drunken Eric is discouraged from leaving the room by the Inspector. This clarifies for us that Eric has something to reveal. His challenge to the *heavy-handed* Inspector allows the Inspector to observe that there is little difference between criminals and respectable citizens.

On returning to the stage, Sheila faces up to her guilt rather better than her father has or than any of the others will. She tells how she has the girl dismissed because she was in a *furious temper*. Although the girl had secretly smiled to another assistant about the unsuitability of a dress that she was trying on, Sheila is big enough to confess that the real reason was that the girl was *very pretty* and suited the dress far better. When the Inspector says, '... *you used the power you had, as the daughter of a good customer and of a man well-known in the town, to punish the girl*' Sheila shows remorse at her action.

Suspicion falls on Gerald

(To end Act 1)

Following Sheila's confession, the Inspector sums up the chain of events so far – Eva Smith was dismissed from Birling and Company because strikes for better wages were not to be repeated, she found and lost a job at a clothes shop because Sheila was angry with herself. The Inspector adds that Eva Smith then became Daisy Renton.

The mention of this name startles Gerald, who has so far been untouched by the inquiry. Leaving the room with Eric, the Inspector looks at the lovers as if to say, 'Now it's your turn to squirm and sort things out between you.' Sheila shows that she knows Gerald well enough to tell that he not only knew the dead woman, but *knew her very well*. Sheila at last has the explanation for his absence the previous summer. It is admitted by Gerald's silence rather than by his confession. He is quick to save his own skin by declaring the affair to have been over for some time, thereby excusing himself from blame. He appeals to Sheila to collude with him in keeping his affair from the Inspector.

As the Act closes, Sheila, the only one to accept and face her portion of the blame, and sense that there is more to come, tells Gerald that she hates *to think how much he knows that we don't know yet*. This also prepares the audience for more revelations and keeps us on the edge of our seats.

On your bike ...

?   What factors could have shaped Sheila's personality in such a way that she behaves so badly towards a pretty shop assistant?

?   Write an extract from Eva Smith's diary for the day of one of her dismissals from employment.

?   Note down some of the clues we are given to show what will be developed later.

now the scene's set, enjoy an interval, and come back fresh to more confessions

A*ct 2*

◆ Tension between Sheila and Gerald – Sheila suspects the Inspector.

◆ Mrs Birling blunders in.

◆ Gerald gives details of his affair.

◆ Sheila breaks off her engagement to Gerald.

◆ Mrs Birling is implicated, Eric agitated.

◆ Mrs Birling gives details of an interview with the girl.

◆ More about the baby's father, revelations.

Tension between Sheila and Gerald – Sheila suspects the Inspector

(To p. 21, Sheila stares at him wonderingly and dubiously)

The break in the action has only been for audience convenience. Sheila seizes on the way that the Inspector is building up to questioning Gerald, making him face up to his part in the death. Gerald veils his desire to keep Sheila from knowing any more about the *unpleasant and disturbing things* with remonstrations that she is too tired to hear any more and should be spared further questioning. The Inspector draws out of Gerald that he is keener to protect Sheila from unpleasantness than he was to protect Daisy Renton with some irony.

More cracks in the relationship between the engaged couple are revealed. Sheila wants to stay and hear all about it. She does not say why, but given her intuitive grasp of the situation so far, it is probably because she thinks it will be better for their relationship if all the details are out in the open. Gerald misses this and thinks she wants to see him squirm as she just has. ❍ What does this say about their relationship?

The Inspector soon adds that Sheila wants to stay so that she will not have to bear all the burden of guilt. At this point Gerald is too preoccupied with his relationship with Sheila to realize that his former mistress has just died.

Sheila then notes, for the first time, that the Inspector is not like any other she has ever met, as if he is a *real one*. In their exchange it is hinted at that he is an inspector of the conscience – a far more real arbiter of guilt or innocence. Only Sheila, and perhaps Eric to a certain degree, feel this.

Mrs Birling blunders in

(To p. 24, Mrs Birling: What is it you want to know?)

Soon, Mrs Birling enters, *quite out of key* with what is going on. At the deeper level this is because she is not troubled by her conscience. Sheila is, however, as indicated by Mrs Birling's observation that the Inspector has made *a great impression* on Sheila. He replies, '*We often do on the young ones,*' suggesting that the hope for social change rests in the hands of the *impressionable* young rather than with their more rigidly-minded elders. Mrs Birling continues to ignore Sheila's pleas not *to build up a kind of a wall between us and that girl* – a wall that exists on many levels.

Insisting on shutting out her conscience, and accusing the Inspector of impertinence, Mrs Birling and the Inspector play on the double meaning of the word 'offence'. She is told that the Inspector (or the conscience) never takes offence. The Inspector uses the word in its legal sense – of a crime committed rather than as an insult, suggesting they discontinue mentions of offences. Sounding just like her husband, Mrs Birling then threatens the Inspector with rank – hinting that he had better go more softly or complaints to his superiors about his *peculiar and offensive manner* may be made. Gerald begins to catch on, and adds to Sheila's attempts to stop her mother from trying to avoid the inquiry. We learn that Eric's conscience is troubling him – he seems to be in *an excitable silly mood*.

At last the pretence about Eric's drink problem comes out. Mrs Birling cannot admit to herself that Eric has such a problem, but Sheila who notes that her brother is *probably in enough trouble already*, tells the truth and is supported in her claim by Gerald, despite Mrs Birling's appeal to him to deny Sheila's assertion. Again Mrs Birling fails to realize that her conscience should be troubled, and that it is not her daughter that is challenging her, it is rather that the Inspector *hasn't started on you yet.*

It is then confirmed that Eric will be taking his turn at being questioned – when the Inspector is ready and not before. All except Eric are present, and we are about to hear the details of Gerald's involvement in the life of the dead woman. ❍ Why do you think Priestley has made sure that Eric is not present for Gerald's confession?

Gerald gives details of his affair

(To p. 27, Sheila moves to the desk)

For the benefit of the Birling parents, who have not heard Sheila's story of the incident in the dress shop, and to recap for the audience, the Inspector outlines the incident. He then shocks the Birling parents as he suddenly asks Gerald when he got to know the woman now known as Daisy Renton. Realizing that he cannot wriggle out of a confession since he is being pressurized by both Sheila and the Inspector, he begins his explanation. Gerald again tries to send Sheila away, but she is angry and determined not to give him an easy time.

It is interesting that Gerald at first refers casually to the bar where the couple met as *the Palace,* and then as *the Palace music hall.* His first mention suggests quite a familiarity with the place, a point picked up by Sheila who notes sarcastically that the gathering *'didn't think you meant Buckingham Palace.'* Later the Inspector calls it *the Palace Variety Theatre.* Places where sex is sold are typically given exotic names. Perhaps by using so many names for the same place, Priestley is suggesting anybar, anyplace.

When you know the play, it is interesting that since Mrs Birling is on a charity committee for deserving cases, she should seem so shocked that prostitutes operate in Brumley. It is probably a case of help being given according to middle class values rather than who really needs it. It would also be in character for Mrs Birling to pretend that prostitutes didn't exist – and to deny things such as Gerald's *disgusting affair.* This is a feature of respectability, a point picked up again later when

53

it emerges that a respected man in the town, Alderman Meggarty, *one of the worst sots and rogues in Brumley* with an *obscene fat carcase*, frequents the bar in search of prostitutes. Soon after, when Sheila mentions knowing a girl whose blouse was torn by the same Alderman Meggarty, the exclamation from her father seems to be more one of surprise that Sheila should know about such things than disgust for a dirty old man.

Sheila adds more irony to the situation when she again insists on being present to hear Gerald's story – the one she points out, in which she is *engaged to the hero of it*. As Gerald describes Daisy Renton, he realizes at last that she is dead. It is as if he has pushed his memories of her to the back of his mind, and has also denied the affair to himself, along with its implications for his involvement in her death and the future of his relationship with Sheila.

In one of the longest uninterrupted passages in the play, Gerald then gives details of how he came to Daisy's rescue, and how she explained that she was alone in the world, unemployed, poor and hungry. Under pressure to continue from Sheila as well as the Inspector, Gerald continues to tell how Daisy was about to be made homeless, that he put her up in a friend's flat, and that she became his mistress. Sheila points out that Gerald should be directing his confession to her and not the Inspector, although of course it is his conscience that he is addressing.

Time out

?   Circle any of the following words which could be used to sum up Sheila's attitude in this part of the play: sarcastic, ironic, happy, angry, jealous, sad, tearful, intuitive, indignant, hysterical, intelligent, naive.

?   How did Gerald distract Alderman Meggarty's attention from the girl?

?   What do the Birling parents expect policemen to do and be like?

now take a break before some implications and agitations

Sheila breaks off the engagement

(To p. 29, Mrs Birling sits below the table)

The tone of Gerald's confession changes as he, Sheila and the Inspector talk of feelings and Gerald explains how the affair ended. ○ When Sheila says, *'That's a nice thing to say'*, in reply to the Inspector's statement that women need someone to love, do you think she means it, or is what she says ironic?

Again the Inspector shows signs of his real identity, or rather lack of it – he gives his own opinion about the need that women have to love and the kind of world we live in. Both the Inspector and Sheila want to know if Gerald was in love with Daisy – a detail that Birling would prefer not to know. He protests, perhaps to try and limit the damage to the relationship of the newly engaged young couple. Again, in a manner not usual in a police officer, the Inspector challenges Birling's right to protest, reminding him of his own hand in the death. Still only Sheila is facing up to her guilty role in the suicide.

Far from *living on the moon*, Sheila is very down-to-earth about the affair. She quickly understands how flattered Gerald must have been by Daisy's attentions, and is quick to point out that she doesn't think much of it, although she does give him some credit for at last being honest. Echoing her husband's sentiments, Mrs Birling tries to halt further discussion of *this disgusting affair*, and is quickly reminded by her daughter that her previous attempts to avoid involvement in the suicide were futile.

Gerald has also begun to face up to his own involvement, offering to tell the Inspector anything else he may want to know. This includes his account of the end of the affair, how well Daisy had taken it, and how bad he felt about it, contrary to Sheila's angry and ironic remark that it must have been nice for Gerald that she took it so well.

The dialogue continues with the information that Gerald gave Daisy some more money to tide her over and that although he didn't know where she had gone, he thought she had left Brumley. With a final note of pathos, which makes Gerald feel really rotten, the Inspector explains that Daisy went to a seaside place to reflect on the affair and grieve for it since she did not expect to be as happy ever again.

As Gerald asks if he can leave to take a walk, Sheila hands back the engagement ring he has given her only an hour or so previously. Sheila then sums up what has happened in their relationship and what she now thinks of her former fiancé. She says that she knew he had lied about his absences the previous summer, but that she has gained a new respect for him. She adds that the revelations about his affair, although partly her fault, as Daisy's unemployment could be traced back to her, meant that they were now different people from the ones they had been only an hour before. Birling's attempt to intervene and make excuses for Gerald are useless, as both the lovers know. Gerald's interview is over, but as he recognizes before he leaves the stage, and in reply to Mrs Birling, the *wretched business* is not over yet.

Mrs Birling implicated, Eric agitated

(To p. 32, Sheila sits in the armchair)

Prompted by Sheila, the Inspector next shows a photograph to a reluctant Mrs Birling, who claims not to recognize it. The Inspector quite bluntly accuses her of not telling the truth, which prompts an angry Birling to demand an apology. The hypocrisy in the polite society that Priestley is presenting to us surfaces again when Birling asserts that he is a public man, with the implication that such office overrules right, truth and justice, and the doing of one's duty as the Inspector is doing. Birling is also reminded that privilege brings responsibility – another new concept for him.

Sheila, probably to remind us of what has been revealed about each character so far, runs through her father's, her own and Gerald's shabby behaviour. She adds that she knows her mother recognized the person in the photograph, and challenges her to tell the truth.

As the door slams and Birling goes to investigate, the Inspector starts on Mrs Birling, who is reluctant to admit first her membership of the Brumley Women's Charity

Organisation, and secondly having been the Chairperson at a meeting held two weeks previously. To foreshadow his poor opinion of her idea of help, the Inspector asks for clarification that the role of the organization is to help women in distress. Mrs Birling's reply, which Priestley is careful to add is said with dignity, is, *'We've done a great deal of useful work in helping deserving cases.'* The key word here is *deserving*, as it hints that the dead woman has had some dealings with this committee but has not been considered deserving.

There is a momentary interruption in which the Birling parents inform us that Eric must have gone out, and is in a strange mood. Their worry about him is entirely unconnected with the Inspector's visit – they know he is unstable, and they assume he is not needed in the inquiry. The Inspector corrects them in this assumption, which prompts *bewildered and rather frightened glances between them*. This lets the audience know that Eric will not be let off the hook, and will be shown to have played a part in the death. Before we have the details of Mrs Birling's involvement, the Inspector reveals the information that she saw the young woman in question just two weeks ago – a revelation which produces an *astonished* Sheila.

Circle the word ...

Put a ring around the correct word in the following statements:

? When Eva Smith appealed to the committee, Mrs Birling was: helpful / passive / prejudiced / neutral.

? When drunk, Eric can turn: queasy / bigoted / around / nasty.

? The Inspector is: provocative / drunk / ashamed / hilarious.

take a break before an interview

Mrs Birling gives details of her interview with the girl

(To p. 34, Birling rises and tries to protest)

It is first revealed that the girl presented herself to the committee as Mrs Birling, not Eva Smith or Daisy Renton. This was interpreted by the real Mrs Birling as *gross impertinence*, and by her own admission this prejudiced her against the girl from the start. She goes on to say that the girl claimed it was simply the first name she thought of. Mrs Birling adds that the rest of the girl's story was a pack of lies – the girl was not married at all. ❂ What do you think Eva's real reason was for saying she was Mrs Birling?

Still refusing to listen to her conscience, Mrs Birling very unwisely states, *'Unlike the other three, I did nothing I'm ashamed of or that won't bear investigation ... I did my duty.'* She also rather obstinately claims that the Inspector has no power, and can put no pressure on her to make her think otherwise. By now the audience is well aware of the way the Inspector can demolish such claims and that her assertion will soon be undermined – it is how it is done that has us gripped in our seats now.

When the Inspector then brings up the image of the dead woman in hospital, the image is made all the more terrible by Sheila prefacing the revelation that the girl was pregnant with a plea to the Inspector not to make her imagine it again.

It is then confirmed that the pregnancy was the reason for the appeal to Mrs Birling's committee – and Priestley makes sure that the audience is quickly informed that Gerald Croft is not the baby's father. ❂ Why do you think this is? The Inspector's invitation to Mrs Birling to add to her account is answered with her shifting responsibility to the baby's father.

The Inspector, in what has now become his characteristic manner, reminds Mrs Birling that she was also responsible – she is guilty of refusing help when it was most needed and influencing others to refuse it. So damning is his assessment of her guilt, that Sheila declares her mother's refusal *cruel and vile*. ❂ Do you agree with her? Birling of course is only concerned with how it will look, particularly to the press. ❂ What do you think Gerald would have said if he had heard this?

Mrs Birling reminds her husband and daughter of their own part in the dead girl's downfall, and then attempts again to justify herself. She claims that she drew the truth from the girl, which meant that since the identity of the father was known, he should be forced to marry or support her. In her typically prejudiced way she dismisses the girl's reasons for not accepting the father's help – and gives the Inspector the next piece of rope with which to hang herself.

More about the baby's father, revelations

(To p. 36 – end of Act 2)

Taking a very firm line with the Birling parents, the Inspector insists on knowing what the woman actually said about the baby's father. We learn that the man is a drunken young waster, who had none the less given her money. Mrs Birling tries to avoid the Inspector's next question about why the woman would take no more money by again moving away and dismissing what was said as nonsense. Under pressure, she eventually reveals that the girl would take no more money because it was stolen. Trying to save her own skin she again says that she didn't believe this story any more than the first one and still believes herself innocent of blame.

The Inspector points out that the girl's appeal to the committee, quite apart from not wanting to accept stolen money, was also to prevent the father from stealing more money and getting into trouble. Mrs Birling, although admitting this possibility, again excuses herself from blame, passing it first to the girl herself and then to the baby's father. The significance of this is not lost on Sheila, who again states her own and her father's culpability, but fails to stop her mother digging a deeper hole for herself.

Priestley cleverly sets up Mrs Birling for a fall by having the Inspector feed back her accusations and prejudices to her, as a question, for her to confirm, Sheila tries to help her, but without success. It soon transpires that the Birling parents must join Sheila in realizing that the father of the dead girl's baby is none other than Eric. Having said that he *should be made an example of*, and that *he ought to be dealt with very severely*, and made to *confess in public his responsibility*, Mrs Birling refuses to believe the truth about her son, who now rejoins the action. With the Inspector having done his duty according to Mrs Birling's standards, with Sheila telling her mother that she begged her to stop, and with a pale and distressed Eric back on stage, the curtain falls on Act 2.

What do you think?

?   What kind of a case do you think Mrs Birling would have considered to be a good one to be put before her committee?

?   Do you agree with the Inspector that *women want somebody to love. It's their weakness*?

?   Make a Mind Map of Gerald's concerns as they might have been in the summer of 1911.

now you know what everyone's done, take a break before the twists, turns and tidying

Act 3

◆ Eric confesses paternity.
◆ Eric admits to 'borrowing' money.
◆ The Inspector sums up.
◆ The Inspector's identity is questioned.
◆ Gerald confirms that the Inspector is a fake.
◆ Gerald pieces together an explanation.
◆ Two important phone calls.

Eric confesses paternity

(To p. 39, Eric does not reply)

The set is the same as for the previous two acts and the action continuous. Imagine you have just returned from a drink at the bar. You are waiting to hear how Eric has contributed to the girl's downfall, and how all the loose ends and blame will be tidied up.

Never in the play have the problems in the family been so clear as now. All the pretence, secrets and lies are out in the open, all the skeletons out of the family cupboard. Mrs Birling, still in denial, however, hopes there is a mistake. She cannot open her eyes to see that her son is less than perfect, insisting that he is *'not that type – you don't get drunk.'* Sheila will not, however, let her get away with it, and Eric has judged his mother's response correctly.

Sheila corrects Eric, who thinks that she must have told their mother about his drinking some time ago. She now insists on the truth, which is such a strange idea to the Birling parents that Mrs Birling cannot understand it and her husband can only see it as disloyalty to the family. Enough is said about loyalty for it not to matter that the Inspector interrupts and tells them they can *adjust* their family relationships when he's gone.

An exchange takes place between the men regarding alcohol once again. Eric is desperate for a drink, Birling is enraged by his request for one, and the Inspector insists that he takes one, *just to see him through.* Birling accepts the Inspector's authoritative insistence, and Eric demonstrates his familiarity with drinking – much to the distaste of the family. It is as if the action gives them a chance to see Eric as he really is, not as they have idealized him.

The Inspector prises the sordid details out of Eric. Like Gerald he met the girl at the Palace bar, when she was hungry and had drunk alcohol on an empty stomach. Eric dismisses any suggestion that the girl had been offering herself as a prostitute, though he mentions *some woman who wanted her to go there* – a remark that is never explained, but implies that the girl was being drawn into organized prostitution. It is quite big of Eric to admit to having the potential to *turn nasty*, to *make a row*, and to having had sex while too drunk to remember anything about it.

The women are sent out of the room, as Eric's tale is judged by Mr Birling to be unfit to be heard by women. ❍ Do you think he is right? Further details of the liaison are related, and as he is reproached by his father, Eric retaliates by exposing the true, unsavoury conduct of Birling's *respectable friends*, and the *fat old tarts* they go around with. Again the Inspector orders them to discuss such matters later.

We hear that the girl didn't want Eric to marry her, that she treated him as if he *were a kid*, despite a similarity in age. Facing up to his responsibility, however, Eric explains that he supplied the unemployed and pregnant girl with money amounting to about £50. Note that this sum represents almost a year's wages at the rate Eva Smith had received from Birling's factory in 1910. Both the Inspector and the angry father want to know where Eric got the money from.

Eric admits to 'borrowing' money

(To p. 41, Inspector: Stop!)

Eric's silence on being asked where he got £50 from is equivalent to a confession of stealing – from his father's own office, though Eric is quick to claim that he intended to pay it back. To make sure we have all paid attention, Birling reminds us that Eric is both responsible for a pregnancy and now stealing, as he tells the women who have just re-entered the room. ❍ How likely do you think it is that Eric would have paid back the money?

We learn that Eric has committed this fraud by collecting small cash sums owed to the company, issuing receipts to the customer to show they have been paid, but removing records of the debt at the office. Still applying the dual standard of one rule for outsiders and another for family, Birling is anxious to cover up the evidence as soon as possible.

As Eric's behaviour is blamed and counter-blamed, the Inspector moves on to hear that the girl would take no more money when she knew it was stolen. Sheila then lets Eric know the part their mother has played in the girl's downfall, and some of the strongest accusations made in the entire play are levelled at Mrs Birling by her son. The atmosphere is now almost hysterical. Eric is *nearly at breaking point*, and it takes the Inspector's loud intervention to defuse the tension.

The Inspector sums up

(To p. 42, He walks straight out ...)

The Inspector instructs the family to remember that *'each of you helped to kill her.'* One by one, he restates the nature of their role in the girl's death. Mrs Birling *turned her away when she most needed help.* Eric *used her for the end of a stupid drunken evening.* Sheila *had her turned out of a job*, and Birling is accused of starting the sorry chain of events by refusing her pay rise and dismissing her. Gerald, who is still absent from the gathering gets off rather lightly, with the comment that *he at least had some affection for her and made her happy for a time.*

Throughout his summing up he reminds the family that they won't forget what they have done and that it is too late to make amends. Again, it is Sheila who shows the most remorse.

The Inspector then makes an extremely strong speech and moves from the particular to the general, pointing out that there are *millions and millions and millions of Eva Smiths and John Smiths* who suffer at the hands of the selfish. In keen contrast to Birling's speech in Act 1 when he talks of everyone for himself, the Inspector, with the moral authority he has argued for himself, strongly states that we have collective responsibility for each other. His final words are very strong indeed, *'... if men will not learn that lesson, then they will be taught it in fire and blood and anguish.'* He leaves the stage for the play's final gear-change.

The Inspector's identity is questioned

(To p. 44, Birling: ... and get to work quickly too)

After the Inspector leaves, the *staring, subdued and wondering* family start the process of arguing, blaming and readjusting their relationships – the process the Inspector has continually prevented them from carrying out while he conducted his investigation. Perhaps not surprisingly, Birling, unable to digest the whole picture of the portions of blame, and equally unable to accept responsibility, either as an individual or collectively, starts off the chain of accusations, centring on Eric.

He shows that he is so small-minded as to be concerned more with the likelihood of scandal and no knighthood than with critical self-examination as a father and employer. He still treats his son like a child, while, ironically, pouring himself a whisky.

The blame then shifts to the Birling parents as Eric counters their criticism of him with criticism of them. Sheila backs him up as Birling tries to belittle the share of the blame levelled at him and his wife. In answer to Sheila's acknowledgment of the gravity of what they have all done, he shows that he views what has happened in terms of the scandal that will arise from it, not the lessons to be learned from the deed itself. Eric reminds his father of the speech he made in Act 1, with the observation that Birling hadn't told the Inspector *that it's every man for himself.*

The discussion then shifts as Sheila seeks confirmation that it was after that speech when the Inspector had called. She and her mother have begun to suspect that the Inspector was not what he seemed, and although there is no suggestion that he is in any way a manifestation of their collective guilt, it is implied by Sheila's observation.

The Birling parents of course seize upon this idea immediately. If the Inspector is not really from the police then they can forget about the whole nasty business. The Birling children, facing up to responsibility, realize that it makes no difference at all. The Inspector, whoever he may be, has made them confess their guilt towards one in several million Eva Smiths.

Birling shows his concern with status again. He simply cannot come to terms with the idea that anyone could accuse a former Lord Mayor and magistrate of anything – with the station comes an immunity to scrutiny, no matter what a person does.

Always more intelligent than the others, Sheila points out that the Inspector wormed his information out of them rather than supplying it. This causes Birling to point out patronizingly that they should all have been more cagey rather than allowing themselves to be bluffed. Mrs Birling shows a woeful lack of moral development in her comment that she did no more than her duty, which makes her daughter sigh with despair. Birling, without acknowledging the benefit of hindsight, refers to the Inspector as a *Socialist or some sort of crank* of the type that he earlier criticized and which has just been mentioned by Eric.

Birling then accuses Eric of not standing up to the Inspector and justifies not doing so himself because of preoccupation with Eric's scandalous behaviour rather than his own. Sheila and Eric know that Birling is fooling himself that he could have seen the Inspector alone. Mrs Birling echoes the idea that loyalty is more important than moral truth in her comment: *'Really, from the way you children talk, you might be wanting to help him instead of us'* and looks to her husband to do something about the situation.

Over to you

? Is loyalty more important that moral truth? What do you think?

? Do you side with the Birling parents or the Birling children?

? Which character do you like most and which do you like least? Why?

take a break – go for a walk like Gerald

Gerald confirms that the Inspector is a fake

(To p. 47, Eric is moving restlessly down L.)

That the family all *look at each other in alarm* when the door bell rings shows how uncomfortable they all are following the evening's proceedings. ❂ Who do you think they think the caller might be? They are relieved that the caller is Gerald returning from his walk. The Birling parents are quick to prevent Sheila from giving any further details of the revelations made after Gerald left, though she does indicate that things worsened.

It is then revealed that the Inspector was a fake, a fact Gerald has uncovered by chatting to a policeman he knows and bumped into when he was out. Extremely pleased with this information, Birling decides to confirm it by telephoning a senior policeman he knows, claiming that he had intended to do this anyway. As he speaks into the telephone, repeating and spelling out the Inspector's name, Goole, we are invited to see the imposter as an apparition, or a ghoul.

Deciding that they have *been had*, or bluffed, as in the scene previous to Gerald's entry, the family continue in their roles – Sheila and Eric facing up to themselves, their parents claiming that it was obvious they were being fooled all along. Still with an eye watchful for scandal, Mrs Birling makes sure Gerald knows no more about their *crimes and idiocies*, as she proudly claims to be the only one *who didn't give in* to the Inspector. Unlike the Birling parents, however, Gerald, although he has uncovered the fake policeman, realizes that the fact of their confessions is still to be resolved.

Gerald pieces together an explanation

(To p. 50, They all watch tensely)

Still treated as a child by his parents, Eric, supported by Sheila, takes over as the moral force on stage. He will not sit down for the sensible, cosy chat that his parents hope to have in order to assess how to limit the damage done. He reveals to Gerald that he stole money, asserts that the girl is still dead because of what they all did to her, and that anything else is a pretence. Sheila says Eric's comments are the *'best thing any one of us has said tonight and it makes me feel a bit less ashamed of us.'*

Juxtaposed with this argument is the Birling view of their children and their actions: *'They just won't try to understand our position or to see the difference between a lot of stuff like this coming out in private and a downright public scandal.'*

As the tension between Eric and his father reaches boiling point, and Eric continues to hit home the fact of the girl's suicide, Gerald questions whether her death is fact. He is prompted again to confess and apologize to Sheila for keeping a mistress, upon which she interestingly says, *'you came out of it better than the rest of us.'* ✪ Do you agree?

Gerald then questions whether they have even been involved with the same girl. He points out that neither Birling, Sheila nor Mrs Birling necessarily saw the same photograph of apparently the same girl and Gerald and Eric did not see a photograph at all. By the time she met the two men she had changed her name, besides which their relationship with her was so intimate that a photograph was not needed to jog their memories, as it was with the others.

They develop the idea that they may have known several different girls, and would therefore not share any collective responsibility or guilt. Eric, however, cannot see that any such explanation can alter his or his mother's role until his father questions whether any girl has died at all. They decide to telephone the hospital to seek confirmation.

Two important phone calls

(To end of play)

Gerald telephones the hospital claiming to be concerned for one of his father's employees who may have committed suicide by drinking disinfectant; the family look on anxiously. To Birling's immense relief, there has been no suicide. He recovers a celebratory air, inviting Gerald to take a drink, and mocking his children for their reaction to the tragedy, despite Sheila pointing out that even though they have been implicated in a hoax, the accusations still stand and a tragedy could have taken place. Thick-skinned and unmoved as ever, Birling tries to persuade Sheila to become engaged to Gerald again, but the Birling children are horrified to see that the others are *pretending everything's just as it was before.*

Sheila protests further that the matter has been anything but a joke and that they should have all learned something from the Inspector regardless of him being a fake. She particularly refers to how the Inspector made her feel when he talked of *Fire, blood and anguish.* Apparently only she and Eric, representing the younger generation so put down by their elders, have developed morally. As they are being slighted for *knowing it all* and not being able to take a joke by Birling, the telephone rings. He answers it and the curtain falls as he tells the others that a police inspector is on his way to ask some questions about a girl who has died on the way to the hospital after drinking some disinfectant.

Although it is never explained, it is fairly clear that Priestley means the audience to understand that the fake Inspector has been a manifestation arising from the collective guilt of the privileged classes at their treatment of those worse off than them – the Eva and John Smiths of the world. The older generation representing the values of the capitalist Empire have refused to learn important lessons about collective responsibility. They are now going to be forced to learn them by a younger generation with more appropriate values.

And finally

?   Who do you think feels more uncomfortable after the curtain falls – the Birling parents or the Birling children?

?   How do you think relationships in the Birling household would change after the evening when the Inspector called?

?   Write a news article that might appear in the Brumley Echo giving details of a scandal involving the Birling family.

now take a break before you review the play

Complete these summaries:

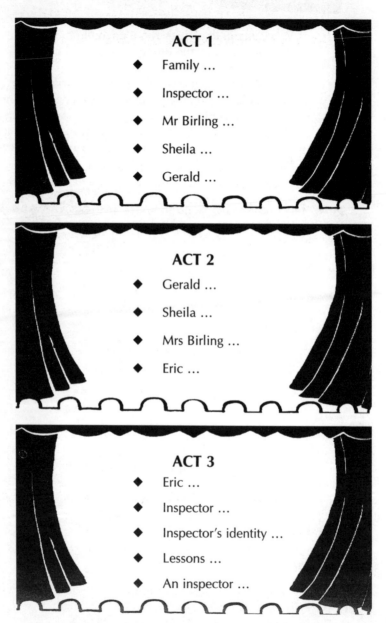

ACT 1
- ◆ Family …
- ◆ Inspector …
- ◆ Mr Birling …
- ◆ Sheila …
- ◆ Gerald …

ACT 2
- ◆ Gerald …
- ◆ Sheila …
- ◆ Mrs Birling …
- ◆ Eric …

ACT 3
- ◆ Eric …
- ◆ Inspector …
- ◆ Inspector's identity …
- ◆ Lessons …
- ◆ An inspector …

You will find the completed summaries on page 5.

TOPICS FOR DISCUSSION AND BRAINSTORMING

One of the best ways to revise is with one or more friends. Even if you're with someone who hardly knows the text you're studying, you'll find that having to explain things to your friend will help you to organize your own thoughts and memorize key points. If you're with someone who has studied the text, you'll find that the things you can't remember are different from the things your friend can't remember – so you'll help each other.

Discussion will also help you to develop interesting new ideas that perhaps neither of you would have had alone. Use a **brainstorming** approach to tackle any of the topics listed below. Allow yourself to share whatever ideas come into your head – however silly they seem. This will get you thinking creatively.

Whether alone or with a friend, use Mind Mapping (see p. vi) to help you brainstorm and organize your ideas. If with a friend, use a large sheet of paper and thick coloured pens.

Any of the topics below could feature in an exam paper, but even if you think you've found one in your actual exam, be sure to answer the precise question given.

BACKGROUND

1 What economic system was in place in 1912 when the play was set?
2 How had this system changed by the time Priestley wrote the play?
3 How are Priestley's life and beliefs reflected in *An Inspector Calls?*

SUMMARY

Look at the summary list of key points below. Number them 1–10 in the right order.

- The Inspector interrogates Mrs Birling. ☐
- They discover that the Inspector is a fake. ☐
- Sheila owns up to her tantrum. ☐
- The police telephone to say an Inspector is on his way. ☐

- The Inspector leaves. ☐
- Sheila gives Gerald back the ring. ☐
- The family are celebrating Sheila and Gerald's engagement. ☐
- Eric confesses to being the father of the dead girl's baby. ☐
- Birling talks of Eva Smith's dismissal. ☐
- Gerald owns up to his affair with the girl. ☐

CHARACTER

1 What evidence in the text can you find to support the view that Birling is a social climber?
2 How do you think Eric might change after the play?
3 Do you think Sheila will marry Gerald after all?
4 Describe these characters in your own words:
   (a) Mrs Birling
   (b) Sheila
   (c) The Inspector.
5 What contribution does Edna make to the play?
6 Who is the morally superior person during the interview at the Brumley Women's Charity Organisation?
7 That the Inspector is not really a policeman makes all the difference. Do you agree?
8 Write Eva Smith's obituary.
9 What sort of husband do you think Gerald would make for Sheila?

Now look at the relationship summary chart.

Relationship Summary

Fill in the boxes with the missing information about Eva's relationship to the other characters.

WHO	RELATIONSHIP	WHEN	WHERE	WHAT
Birling		2 years ago		
Mrs Birling				
Sheila			Milwards	
	Lover/ mistress			
Eric				Penniless pregnancy

LANGUAGE

1 What is the significance of Eva Smith's name?
2 What is the significance of the Inspector's name?
3 What devices does Priestley give the Inspector to ensure that the inquiry goes *one person and one line of enquiry at a time*?
4 List the modern or 'slang' words that are used in the play. Who uses them?
5 What effect do the door banging and the door bell ringing have on the play?
6 What is the difference between 'plot' and 'theme'? Give examples.

THEMES

1 What part does alcohol play in *An Inspector Calls*?
2 How does Priestley explore time?
3 What part is played by young people in the play?
4 In Act 2 (p. 27) the Inspector says the world is a *battlefield rather than a home*. Do you agree with him?
5 Make up a list of rules that women applying to Mrs Birling's charity committee should follow to be eligible to apply for help. How would your list compare?
6 How do the attitudes of the men in the play alter towards young women of different social standing?

Solution to crossword on page 45

HOW TO GET AN 'A' IN ENGLISH LITERATURE

In all your study, in coursework, and in exams, be aware of the following:

- **Characterization** – the characters and how we know about them (e.g. what they say and do, how the author describes them), their relationships, and how they develop.
- **Plot and structure** – what happens and how it is organized into parts or episodes.
- **Setting and atmosphere** – the changing scene and how it reflects the story (e.g. a rugged landscape and storm reflecting a character's emotional difficulties).
- **Style and language** – the author's choice of words, and literary devices such as imagery, and how these reflect the mood.
- **Viewpoint** – how the story is told (e.g. through an imaginary narrator, or in the third person but through the eyes of one character – 'She was furious – how dare he!').
- **Social and historical context** – influences on the author (see 'Background' in this guide).

Develop your ability to:

- Relate **detail** to **broader content, meaning and style**.
- Show understanding of the author's **intentions, technique and meaning** (brief and appropriate comparisons with other works by the same author will gain marks).
- Give **personal response and interpretation**, backed up by **examples** and short **quotations**.
- **Evaluate** the author's achievement (how far does the author succeed and why?)

Make sure you:

- Know how to use **paragraphs** correctly.
- Use a wide range of **vocabulary** and **sentence structure**.
- Use **short** appropriate **quotations** as evidence of your understanding of that part of the text.
- Use **literary terms** to show your understanding of what the author is trying to achieve with language.

THE EXAM ESSAY

You will probably have about an hour for one essay. It is worth spending about 10 minutes planning it. An excellent way to do this is in the three stages below.

1 **Mind Map** your ideas, without worrying about their order yet.
2 **Order** the relevant ideas (the ones that really relate to the question) by numbering them in the order in which you will write the essay.
3 **Gather** your evidence and short quotes.

You could remember this as the **MOG** technique.

Then write the essay, allowing five minutes at the end for checking relevance, and spelling, grammar and punctuation. **Stick to the question**, and always **back up** your points with evidence in the form of examples and short quotations. Note: you can use '. . .' for unimportant words missed out in a quotation.

Model answer and plan

The next (and final) section consists of a model answer to an exam question on *An Inspector Calls*, together with the Mind Map and essay plan used to write it. Don't be put off if you don't think you could write an essay as good as this one yet. You'll develop your skills if you work at them. Even if you're reading this the night before the exam, you can easily memorize the MOG technique in order to do your personal best.

The model answer and plan are good examples to follow, but don't learn them by heart. It's better to pay close attention to the wording of the question you choose to answer in the exam, and allow Mind Mapping to help you to think creatively.

Before reading the answer, you might like to do a plan of your own to compare with the example. The numbered points, with comments at the end, show why it's a good answer.

QUESTION

Who is most responsible for the death of Eva Smith?

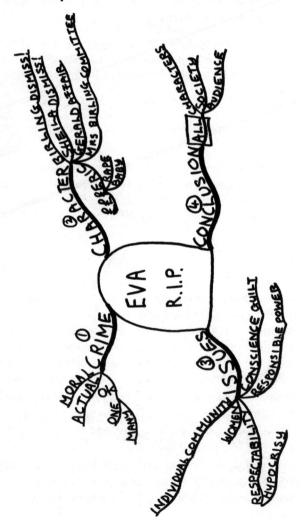

EVA R.I.P.

② CHARACTERS
- REFERS
- ARTHUR BIRLING — DISMISS!
- SHEILA — DISMISS!
- GERALD — AFFAIR
- MRS BIRLING — COMMITTEE
- ERIC — RAPE / BABY

④ CONCLUSION
- ALL CHARACTERS
- ALL SOCIETY
- AUDIENCE

① MORAL / ACTUAL CRIME
- ONE OF MANY
- INDIVIDUAL / COMMUNITY

③ ISSUES
- CONSCIENCE / GUILT
- RESPONSIBLE / POWER
- WOMEN
- RESPECTABILITY
- HYPOCRISY

PLAN

1 Kind of crime committed (suggested/actual, one/many girls, point Priestley is making).
2 Examine each character's part in death (in Priestley's order).
3 Wider issues (developed by themes rather than characters).
4 Conclusion – all characters responsible/society responsible.

ESSAY

To examine the question of which character is most responsible for Eva Smith's death, it is necessary first to look at the kind of crime which has been committed, at the girl herself, and why Priestley wants us to think about who is responsible.

For the greater part of the play, we believe that Eva Smith has killed herself by drinking poison. No character in the play is responsible for the death in the way that a traditional 'whodunnit' would portray. For example, no character actually makes her drink poison. Neither would any character be held responsible for the death in a court of law. The crime is therefore a moral one – and it is in this arena that it is examined.[1] A further complication takes place in the closing lines when the characters are left to examine their own consciences for a death which in one minute has taken place, in the next is a hoax, and in the next takes place again, seemingly real after all.[2]

The play revolves around the Inspector's investigation of the events leading up to Eva Smith's death. Only in the last act is this notion challenged – the Inspector is a fake, and the idea is presented to us that Eva Smith may be more than one girl. Perhaps Priestley gave her such a name to suggest this – Eva, or Eve was the first woman, and stands for all women, Smith is a common name and a symbol for many 'Eva Smiths and John Smiths'.[3]

These factors combine to form the point Priestley is trying to make in this play – that society must change from one in which class conflict, inequality and injustice is commonplace, into a fair society which functions by collective responsibility. This is very much the political and social ideal that the humanitarian Priestley believed in and sought to achieve in much of his writing.[4]

So who is responsible for Eva Smith's death? First we hear of Arthur Birling's part in it. He dismissed her from his factory for asking for fair wages, tossing her out into an unsympathetic world to look for work. She recovers from this setback, and gets a new job, only to suffer outrageous treatment from his daughter Sheila, who cannot bear to see someone look prettier in a dress than she does. Losing her job because the shop cannot lose the Birlings as customers, Eva Smith is given a harder knock from which it is far harder to recover.

The young woman's downfall is slowly but surely taking place by the time she meets Gerald Croft. She survives for a time through the kindness he shows to her while meeting his own sexual motives. By the time their affair is over, she has become dangerously close to the only option left to her by which she could earn a living, prostitution. Although her next sexual encounter that we know about, with Eric Birling, is not for payment, she becomes pregnant, but will not accept money stolen by him to support her. He has treated her 'as if she were an animal, a thing, not a person'.[5] She has hit rock bottom, a place from which it will be very difficult to recover.

The final blow comes from the mean-spirited and prejudiced Sybil Birling. She dislikes the girl so much for using her name, and generally not fitting her value system, that she ignores Eva's desperate situation and dismisses her as undeserving of help from the charity she strongly influences.[6]

Each incident as it is unravelled seems to reveal a deeper responsibility for the death of the girl. Yet each character's role in Eva's downfall is like a piece in a jigsaw. It is the sum of all the different parts which proves to present the insurmountable obstacles from which there is no way out except suicide. In apportioning these degrees of responsibility to characters who have acted out of self-interest in a crime which exists on a moral rather than legal plane, Priestley is blaming society as a whole. Each individual is a part of a community, as the Inspector says in his summing up, 'We don't live alone. We are members of one body. We are responsible for each other.'[7]

In this way Priestley knits the actions of his characters together with the themes he has written the play to address: that community is more important than the individual, that misuse of power, combined with prejudice, hypocrisy and respectability are the ugly pillars supporting an unjust society.[8] He leaves his pre-war characters to examine their guilty consciences with a warning to audiences who have witnessed two World Wars and should therefore be convinced of the validity of his message, '... the time will soon come, when, if men will not learn that lesson, then they will be taught it in fire and blood and anguish.'[9]

In considering who is most responsible for the death of Eva Smith therefore, it must be concluded that all of the characters share the burden of guilt, despite the different degrees to which they can be blamed. However, Priestley is using these characters to demonstrate a possible scenario that grows out of his wider, philosophical conviction – that everyone is responsible for the well-being or otherwise of everyone else in society, regardless of the factors which make us selfish as individuals. In writing a play with such a far-reaching and global message he has sought to teach his audiences the same lesson as he is insisting that his characters learn. They are just lucky to witness, rather than experience, a scenario to demonstrate it.[10]

WHAT'S SO GOOD ABOUT IT?

1 Shows understanding of the play's central themes and issues.
2 Demonstrates sophisticated understanding and knowledge of text.
3 Shows ability to tackle issues.
4 Clear understanding of historical, political and social context of play and of author's beliefs.
5 Good use of a relevant quotation.
6 Shows understanding of the chronology of events and their significance.
7 Good grasp of detail, ability to analyse.
8 Understanding of themes and the way they relate to character.
9 Appreciation of dramatic techniques/apt quotation.
10 Conclusion shows mature overview of play.

More essay plans

QUESTION

Who learns most from an evening with the Inspector?

PLAN

- Priestley makes Inspector set out to teach all characters a lesson and to warn audience (community/individual).
- Younger generation more receptive than old.
- Old don't learn because of old values, self-interest (status, power) – Birling parents.
- Young more in touch and ready to change – Sheila and Eric.
- Gerald 'goes with the flow'.
- Audience also there to learn.
- Conclusion: as characters the younger generation learn most. As audience we must all learn.

QUESTION

Comment on the purpose and approach of the Inspector.

PLAN

- Inspector works on two levels – policeman/interrogator, moralist/voice of conscience.
- Description, significance of name.
- Style of interrogation (sequence, drawing out confessions directly/indirectly, supplying little information, opinions, recaps of characters' actions, use of gruesome imagery).
- Clues to suggest fake policeman, manifestation of conscience.
- Conclusion – moral force.

QUESTION

How does Priestley's use of time relate to events in *An Inspector Calls?*

PLAN

- Time an important device in play/about play.
- Action continuous over three acts – suspense.

- Revelations told as flashbacks, time twist at end of play.
- Play written after two wars, but set before.
- Conclusion – time used for dramatic effect/to make play's message more forceful.

FURTHER QUESTIONS

Here are some more essay questions of the type you can expect to see on an exam paper. Try drawing a Mind Map for each one. Then compare notes with a friend who has done the same.

- How far is it true to say that Sheila is the Inspector's accomplice?
- Who, in your opinion, is the most unsympathetic character in *An Inspector Calls*, and why?
- Priestley once said, '... we must stop thinking in terms of property and power and begin thinking in terms of community and creation.' How far is this conviction reflected in *An Inspector Calls*?

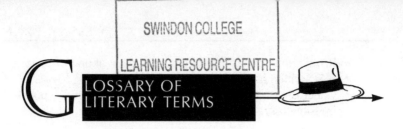

GLOSSARY OF LITERARY TERMS

alliteration   repetition of a sound at the beginnings of words, e.g. *ladies' lips.*

context   the social and historical influences on the author.

dramatic irony   where the audience knows something not known by one, or some, of the characters, e.g. when Birling calls the *Titanic* unsinkable.

foreshadowing   an indirect warning of things to come, often through imagery.

image   a word picture used to make an idea come alive; e.g. a **metaphor**, **simile**, or **personification** (see separate entries).

imagery   the kind of word picture used to make an idea come alive.

irony   (1) where the author or a character says the opposite of what they really think, or pretends ignorance of the true facts, usually for the sake of humour or ridicule; (2) where events turn out in what seems a particularly inappropriate way, as if mocking human effort.

metaphor   a description of a thing as if it were something essentially different but also in some way similar.

personification   a description of something (e.g. fate) as if it were a person.

prose   language in which, unlike verse, there is no set number of syllables in a line, and no rhyming.

setting   the place in which the action occurs, usually affecting the atmosphere; e.g. the Birling's home.

simile   a comparison of two things which are different in most ways but similar in one important way; e.g. 'He fled like a scared rabbit.'

structure   how the plot is organized.

theme   an idea explored by an author; e.g. time.

viewpoint   how a story is told; e.g. through action, or in discussion between minor characters.

INDEX

Page references in bold denote major character or theme sections

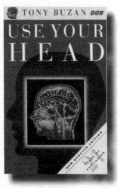

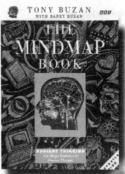